Your
Next
Act

Your Next Act

THE **6 GROWTH ACCELERATORS** FOR CREATING A BUSINESS YOU'LL LOVE FOR THE REST OF YOUR LIFE

MIKE KOENIGS

A Superpower Accelerator Book

Your Next Act

Copyright © 2022 by Mike Koenigs. All rights reserved.

No part of this publication may be reproduced, stored in a retrieval system, or transmitted in any form or by any means, including information storage and retrieval systems, without written permission of the author.

Limit of Liability/Disclaimer of Warranty: The advice and strategies contained herein may not be suitable for your situation. You should consult with a professional where appropriate. All income examples are just that, examples. They are not intended to represent or guarantee you will achieve similar results. Neither the publisher nor the author shall be liable for any loss of profit or any other commercial damages, including but not limited to special, incidental, consequential, or other damages.

For bulk copies of this book or general information on other products and services by Mike Koenigs, please contact VIP@PaidForLife.com

Publishing services by Niche Pressworks, Indianapolis, IN

ISBN: Paperback   978-1-959169-00-0
       eBook   978-1-959169-01-7

Printed in the United States of America.

TABLE OF CONTENTS

3-Day Superpower Accelerator Workshop ·············· vii
How You Can Use This Book ························ ix

Intro Your Category of One Business ················ 1
Ch. 1 Accelerating Growth with the 6Ms ············· 7
Ch. 2 Mindset: How to Win at Business and Life ······ 23
Ch. 3 Market: Claiming Your Turf ·················· 37
Ch. 4 Model: What's Your Brand Promise, What Transformation Do You Deliver, and How Do You Make Money? ····························· 53
Ch. 5 Message: Tell a Powerful Story ················ 67
Ch. 6 Media: Fish Where the Fish Are Biting ·········· 83
Ch. 7 Multipliers: Taking the Accelerators to Another Level ····························· 97
Ch. 8 Next Steps for Your Category of One Brand ···· 109

Meet Mike Koenigs ································ 115
Book Mike Koenigs to Speak ······················· 117
Join the Mastermind ····························· 119
Get Your 10X Multiplier Blueprint ·················· 120

3-Day Superpower Accelerator Workshop

READY FOR MORE FREEDOM? PURPOSE? INCOME?

Reinvent your business and your life... **FAST** with Mike Koenigs' Superpower Accelerator Workshop.

LET'S MAKE YOUR NEXT ACT YOUR BEST ACT.

SUPERPOWER ACCELERATOR

MikeKoenigs.com/Go

HOW YOU CAN USE THIS BOOK

All books in our Superpower Accelerator series have been especially designed and written so you can interact with the content in a variety of ways. Whether you just want a quick graphical overview, a deep dive, or the ability to share the contents with a team member or colleague, we've got you covered.

TEXT 1-1/2 Hours *(1 hour if you cheat and don't do the scorecards!)*	Don't let the brevity of this book fool you; it includes life- and business-changing content, distilled to the most important points so you can read it in one sitting.
GRAPHICS AND ILLUSTRATIONS 20 Minutes	The professionally-designed graphics will hit the main points of the text, serving as a great overview or reminder.
AUDIO Two Hours	Download the audio at MikeKoenigs.com/NextAct and get the complete text AND exclusive commentary and additional insight.
VIDEO 30 Minutes	The supplemental video content will deepen your understanding with additional insights and interviews from the author.

INTRODUCTION

YOUR CATEGORY OF ONE BUSINESS

Do you know who RULES are for?
Other people.
The same goes for lines.
I don't stand in lines. I find the backdoor through a hidden alley behind the building, walk into the greenroom, and start a conversation with the star.

That's a shortcut. I'll pay a premium for shortcuts and time-savers. Hopefully you resonate with these ideas.

After almost four decades as an entrepreneur, business founder, and consultant at the highest levels, I have come to a conclusion:

The worst thing a business can be is a "me too" business and live in the world of the status quo.

In other words, you never want your business to be an imitation or copycat.

When all you are is a tribute band playing someone else's hits, your success level is capped. Led Zepagain will never sell more records than the original. They're at the mercy of someone else to develop new songs and prep the market. In other words, they're stuck — a sentiment I hear far too often from the business owners I talk with.

Here's what I tell them: it's far better for people to hate you than to face irrelevance. I can work with hatred. But passivity and disregard? That's tough to overcome.

Think about businesses, people, or organizations who are so distinct they are in a category all their own, what I call a *Category of One*:

- Elon Musk
- Apple
- Tony Robbins
- Oprah Winfrey
- The New York Yankees
- Ozzy Osbourne
- Donald Trump
- Lululemon
- Amazon
- Chick-Fil-A
- Martha Stewart
- Beyoncé
- JayZ
- Harley-Davidson

Category of One:

Say "**Martha**" or "**Ozzy**," or "**Tony**," and pretty much everyone knows what you're talking about.

Elon Musk
Apple
Tony Robbins
Oprah Winfrey
The New York Yankees
Ozzy Osbourne
Donald Trump
Lululemon
Amazon
Chick-Fil-A
Martha Stewart
Beyoncé
JayZ
Harley-Davidson

Stating your non-negotiable personal or brand values clarifies a mission worth following; a premise worthy of being a part of; a mass movement that merits attention and loyalty.

Say "Martha" or "Ozzy" or "Tony" and pretty much everyone knows what you're talking about. Love them or hate them, you've definitely heard of them. They have defined their own category, and they own that space to the extent they don't really have any competition. They are in a category of their own. (Don't believe me? Drive by any Chick-fil-A anywhere in the country and count the cars in line at the drive-thru... except on Sunday!)

> **When you have a *Category of One* business, you have name recognition, momentum, and leadership.**

You are unusual, and you stand out. People look to you to set the tone. Many times, they will accept no substitute. Anything you touch is instantly worth 3X-10X more and in less time.

Customers and clients approach you, prequalified, saying *"I already know I want to work with you. How do we start?"*

That's what I want for you — a figurative line out the door for your products and services. People begging you to take their money. Rabid fans who get your logo tattooed on their butt. (Hey, whatever floats your boat. I don't judge.)

You might be thinking that creating your own category is impossible because you are in a saturated market or because there's not anything unique about you.

Screw that.

This works whether you're B2C, B2B, large, small, online, or bricks-and-mortar. It doesn't matter if you're a consultant, a retailer, a subject matter expert, a coach, or a ballet teacher. I don't care if you live in New York, New Delhi, or Newfoundland.

After advising and selling products and services to over 161,000 business owners, I can accurately say that every business is unique in its own way. Whether it's what you do, how you do it, or why you do it, there's something different about you.

It's a conundrum: You're special, but your market might not *know* you're special. In fact, not enough of your ideal customers know you exist — or care or understand what makes you unique and valuable.

Here's the real issue: very few businesses ever establish strong brands that get attention, are packaged, positioned, or have a replicable message that makes your ideal customer willing to pay three-to-five times more for your product or service and gives you huge multiples when you choose to sell someday.

More than that, what nearly every business lacks is *sizzle for their steak*. You might be the best thing in the world, but you're packaged and positioned incorrectly and, as a result, **BORING**.

In contrast, sizzle, as one of my favorite clients put it, can 10X the value of an offer, making it the highest ROI investment available to any business owner.

That's what I'll teach you to discover and sharpen in this short guide.

I'm going to introduce you to a straightforward yet powerful framework that will help you determine your *Category of One* brand. You'll need to do some work, but it will be well worth it. Define your *Category of One,* and you're on the way to business success at levels you may never have imagined.

Let's get going,
Mike
☺

P.S. As with most of the content I create, I wrote this book for myself. As a result, sometimes I use language that some might find offensive or too blunt. I polarize on purpose to get a reaction and push buttons. Use that to your advantage. As you're reading, if you get "triggered," ask yourself why. Did I hit a nerve of truth? If so, look for a deeper lesson. Or you can just write me off as an insensitive jerk. I'm okay with that, too.

CH. 1

ACCELERATING GROWTH WITH THE 6MS

I've been called a business alchemist and "SizzleMaker" because of my ability to turn a so-so business into entrepreneurial gold (I've actually been called many less flattering things, but let's set those aside for now). Spend a few days with me in my magic condo on the beach in La Jolla, and you'll emerge with a brand-new product or business identity and a step-by-step plan to 10X your profits, an upgraded offer, sales decks, collateral, videos, articles, lead generation, scripts, and sales systems you need to go out and close deals the next day. Really.

In recent years, I've doubled down on my ability to create transformation in just days for my clients. Not only is it a shit-ton of fun (and lucrative) for me, but it's also impressive to others — both those undergoing the transformation and those who observe it, including spouses and partners, customers, and team members.

It's not surprising. After all, our culture is obsessed with transformation. *Kitchen Nightmares, Hoarders, The Biggest Loser, Extreme Makeover: Home Edition...* we love seeing someone or something go from zero to hero in the course of a 30-minute TV show.

What the show hosts don't talk about so much is the **process** that they use to plot the status quo, diagnose issues, and map a plan for change. The drama is in the before-and-after, not in the details of the undertaking. After all, if you see how the sausage is made, some of the magic might disappear.

But any change agent, whether it's a personal trainer, a cosmetic surgeon, or a home remodeling contractor, must have a tested, repeatable system in order to create successful results week after week. A fitness pro will look at strength, flexibility, diet, and a host of other factors to see where the deficiencies are and prescribe a plan for change. Business transformation is no different. I look at the business's and individual's strengths, weaknesses, and potentials, and then chart a path forward.

I've developed a simple yet robust framework of six Growth Accelerators — a set of underlying principles that serve as a guiding light for solving virtually every challenge you'll ever confront as an entrepreneur. Yeah, that's a big promise, and I stand behind it.

I've used this system to:

- Reinvent America's 401(k) Coach, Charlie Epstein, as a stand-up comedian with his own one-man show, "The Yield of Dreams;"
- Create "The Lifestyle Investor" brand and offering for Justin Donald, who was a previous unknown and now has one of the best and largest brands in the investing and financial categories — and grew from $0 to $15 million in revenue in less than three years;
- Help a well-known fundraiser, Gui Costin, transform existing intellectual property into a multimillion-dollar, hands-off revenue stream;
- Enable an up-and-coming entrepreneur, Coran Woodmass, to evolve into a new version of who he serves, how he works, and what he does; move from $7,000 to $75,000 offers; generate 26 leads in 48 hours; and close deals in a single call;
- Springboard interior designer Connie Wittich into an entirely new brand as the purveyor of "The DNA of Elevated Living," which now has her winning 90 percent of her business pitches and added an additional $6,000,000 in revenue in a single year;
- Recreate an eight-figure franchisor, Joey Osborne, as an advisor to other entrepreneurs hoping to sell their businesses (and save him from the boredom of retirement);
- Repackage and reposition Michael Chu's coaching program, increase the price to $50,000, and generate $1,200,000 in revenue in a single day;
- And hundreds more.

In a word, the 6M Growth Accelerators simply *work*. The process is so powerful and effective that it can bring success to virtually any business — even those that look less-than-promising at first glance.

Let's run through the 6 Ms now, and then in the remainder of the book, we'll do a deep dive on each so you can see how they work.

#1: MINDSET: What matters most?

I love money as much as the next poor kid raised in a rural town of 763 in Minnesota, but money's not why I do what I do.

A cancer diagnosis and near-death experience have shown me that more than anything, purpose comes from creating support, contribution, and collaboration. I'm so committed to the importance of Mindset that I start each of my Superpower Accelerator sessions by focusing on it. While everyone is slightly different, a successful business must be built on a positive, expansive, abundance Mindset. It really is the engine that powers any business, choosing where you go and how high you'll fly. Your non-negotiable values become your brand's values that determine who will work for you and what kind of clients you attract.

You've heard the statement about being the composite of the five people you surround yourself with. While it's not that formulaic, it is founded in truth.

Proof: Have you ever seen an asshat surrounded by really nice, cool people? Probably not too often, because douchebags usually travel in packs. We attract what and who we are — and who we are rubs off on those around us. And that's why it's critical to guard our mindset. It's way too easy to become influenced by the jerks, small thinkers, and naysayers around us.

One way to avoid getting pulled off track is to explicitly state what you value and believe, what I call your non-negotiables. When you do so, you're creating a filter for the opportunities, circumstances, and people you allow into your world. You are clarifying your *Hell Yeahs* and *Hell Nos*.

When you know what you won't tolerate (lack of integrity, backbiting, general pain-in-the-ass-ness), it's easy to avoid it. In fact, in recent years I've told my team that I will not tolerate anyone with an aggravation level of more than five percent. Yes, this is totally and completely objective — but that's the beauty of owning my own business. I get to choose who I work with and often more importantly, who I won't. My energy is simply too precious to spend with people who bother or annoy me. More importantly, I've found that when I eliminate one a-hole from my life, there's now room for five amazing people. My quality of life and my income skyrocket.

I've seen too many entrepreneurs who are failing to get the results they want because they're out of alignment with their clients or customers, their team members, or even their family members. Becoming crystal clear on your Mindset — including your non-negotiable values, your priorities, and your wants and needs — allows you to easily see where the clinkers are.

Clarifying your must-haves and won't-evers can often be enough to create momentum for change. A change in Mindset

Accelerating Growth with the 6Ms

As entrepreneurs, we all want the freedom to choose who we work with — and when and how we work with them — to multiply our influence, income, and impact. The 6 Growth Accelerators provide a proven roadmap to combine your superpower with your passion, and then focus and frame it in a way that grabs attention, generates trust, and influences the right people to take positive action. In short, they provide a way to monetize value in your business that you don't yet see.

#1: MINDSET

What are the non-negotiable beliefs and core values that drive you and your business?

You must consciously manage and direct your mindset to get the results you want.

#2: MARKET

Who do you want to be an inspiration to?

You must understand your perfect ideal customer profile —the top 2% of your best clients — and repel those who are not a match.

#3: MODEL

How do you make money?

You must have a clear brand promise and a system to turn your intellectual property into products that help solve your clients biggest problems and get what they want most.

The Dan Sullivan Question®, (a Strategic Coach® concept) - If you and I were to meet one to three years from today, what would have happened personally and professionally for you to feel happy with your progress? Why did you become an entrepreneur and a business owner in the first place? Was it freedom, freedom of time, money, relationship, and purpose?

#4: MESSAGE

How do you connect with your ideal prospects so that they instantly know who you are, why they should trust you and care about your products and services, and what you are going to do for them?

You must be able to communicate clearly and effectively in the fewest number of words possible to grab their attention, build trust, create credibility, and influence them.

#5: MEDIA

What type of media do your ideal prospects trust and use the most?

You must have an effective and efficient way to get your message in the right formats and in front of the right people.

#6: MULTIPLIERS

What strategics and tactics best leverage the first five Growth Accelerators (M's)?

You must execute effectively to gain leverage, build momentum, and amplify your results. The better your accelerators and the more multipliers you use, the bigger and better your brand reach, results, and impact will be.

can quite literally change your world — or at least the way you experience and interact with the world around you.

What is more fundamental than knowing what your business could become… and then stepping into the role of creator of that potentiality? It's the Prime Directive, and all tactics, strategies, and actions stem from it. Get this wrong, and you're screwed.

Make no mistake. Mindset is not only creating a filter through which to screen opportunities. It's not just "thinking positive." Mindset is so foundational that it will affect real, objective, external market attraction and differentiation for your business.

Stating your values as an individual and as a business entity puts a stake in the ground. It tells people who you are and what they can expect. It gives them a reason to care.

In the Mindset section, I'm going to give you one of the most profound and useful tools I have ever discovered for mapping out values. Not only will you define what they are, but you will also clarify the degree and extent to which you demonstrate them. By being able to measure your values and beliefs, you will become an unstoppable marketer, market maker, and brand builder. And as a bonus, I'm including my own non-negotiables that you can copy-paste for your own business.

#2: MARKET: Who do you want to be an inspiration to?

Your Market is more than just who you sell to. In fact, I want you to stop thinking *transactionally* and start think-ing ***transformationally***.

Your audience is everyone associated with your brand. Your clients and customers, of course. But also your employees, affiliates, and vendors. It's affinity groups like influencers and ambassadors. It could even encompass your competitors (though with your *Category of One* brand, you won't *have* any competitors).

Let's get something straight. You aren't in the business of selling a product. A vending machine can do that. Instead, you are in the business of transformation. What transformation do you provide to those you serve? You take what the great copywriter Eugene M. Schwartz described as "the hopes, dreams, fears and desires that already exist in the hearts of millions of people," and you perform your own brand of voodoo to channel, and hopefully fulfill, that desire.

Once you identify your Market, you need to excavate their deep-seated desires, fears, aspirations, repulsions, wants, problems, and buying behavior. From demographics to psychographics, you want to know as much about them as you can so you can better serve them. Equally important is who you do NOT want to serve (see my 5% Rule in the previous section).

Once you nail this, the next steps take care of themselves.

#3: MODEL: What's your brand promise, what transformation do you deliver, and how do you make money?

Your Model not only determines what and how you provide results, it also determines how you'll get paid for the transformation you're providing. One hint: the way you've always done things may be the very thing you need to abandon in order to move forward.

Simpler and Fewer Doesn't Mean Less. Read that over and over again. This one idea can change your life and business for the better. I wish I had understood and implemented this sooner.

Many times, I see businesses whose processes look like a flowchart for a rocket launch, with hundreds of steps, sub-parts, and extraneous elements. Often these were added over time as a response to a request from one particular customer or client (who likely is high on the aggravation scale). Or they were caused by a minutia-driven team-member who would rather create rules than get something done. I've poked and prodded enough to be familiar with the answers: "Oh, we added part five, section 10, substep 92 because we once had a client who didn't know how to open a PDF, so we mailed them a hard copy."

Stay in business long enough and the exceptions will bog you down, slow you down, and bring you down. Instead, you need to create a simple structure that adheres to the 80-20 rule, giving the biggest bang for the buck without bending yourself into pretzel shapes for the outliers. In fact, I often tell my clients, "Your first job will be to give your team the right to fire the lowest 20 percent of your customers to eliminate the morons who make your team's life hell. This will immediately get rid of 80 percent of your problems and increase your revenue by 50 percent."

One point of clarification: when I talk about Model, I'm referring to both the deliverable *and* the system. You're selling a transformation, but you need to have a repeatable process that allows you to generate that outcome over and over again. It's three steps to X, five elements to Y. It's the unique, elegant, *simple* solution that provides the desired outcome to your customers each and every time.

#4: MESSAGE: What do you need to say to your ideal market so they are ready to work with you? What do they need to hear, to believe, to know to make a buying decision *right now*?

What are the fewest words your perfect customer needs to hear to say "Yes!" and pay in full right now? Your Message is what your ideal market needs to hear from you. It is everything from the language you use to convey your unique advantage, to your company name, website URL, headlines on your landing pages, body copy, scripting in your videos, your blog posts, the title of your books, reports, subject lines, email copy, and more. It even goes beyond the words you use and encompasses the colors, graphics, and other elements that identify you and your offer.

If you have a strong *Category of One* brand, just having something "new" can trigger a buying decision. When U2, Kanye, or Beyoncé releases a new album, past listeners buy because they're anchored into the brand. You might think you're different, but that's a massive mistake. Whether you're selling something for $10 or $10,000,000, the fundamental rules of business are the same.

The best messaging taps into the conversation that is already going on in your ideal client's mind. When you are so zeroed in on who they are and what they want and need, you can seamlessly address desires and pains they may not even have verbalized. You know you've hit it when a prospect looks at you with surprise and says, "Geez, it's like you're reading my mind." Because in a sense, you are.

Every buying decision requires that you present value, overcome objections, create trust and authority, and overcome the fear of doing something wrong or making a bad decision. And that's the logic side! Before you can get there, you have to win the emotional game first.

I'm going to give you a variety of different templates and models so you can develop eye-catching, pupil-dilating, money-making messaging — all of which comes out of knowing your Mindset, Market, and Model. You'll see that when you effectively map those three elements, your messaging has a way of writing itself and you just have to get out of the way.

#5: MEDIA: Where are your ideal clients and how do you reach them?

Do your customers listen to podcasts, watch YouTube, go to live events, or read *Forbes*, *Fast Company*, or *Entrepreneur* magazine? Media is a conduit for delivering a message. It's a tool for getting your Message into the ears, eyes, minds, and hearts of the people in your Market.

These days, there is a shit-ton of attention (and money) paid to building a platform. Entrepreneurs are constantly deluged with offers on leveraging LinkedIn, becoming TikTok famous, getting millions of followers on [insert social media platform du jour]. But a lot of that is smoke and mirrors. In fact, it's 99 percent B.S. You can spend a lot of money to become one of the top accounts on Instagram and still not make any money. Facebook will gladly take hundreds of thousands of dollars and deliver not a single paying customer.

That's because social media platforms are soulless black holes. They exist only to feed themselves. Getting a "following" on any of them is meaningless unless:

1. Those who follow you are your ideal Market.
2. They take action on the offers in front of them.
3. You get them off that platform and put them in your system, because…
4. Social platforms aren't your friends any more than the IRS or politicians are!

Don't make this more complicated than it is. Media either works — meaning it delivers your message from point A (you) to point B (Market) in a way that profitably repays the investment — or it does not.

Check your ego at the door. At the end of the day, who cares how big your platform is or how many followers you have if you're making money? What you really want is the end result, and you want it in a way that is profitable.

I can't tell you how many influencers I know with 10,000, 100,000, 1 million "followers" who turn against them as soon as they make an offer. Followers are irrelevant unless they're paying customers. Show me your bank account, not your Instagram followers.

#6: MULTIPLIERS: What are the strategies and tactics that we can leverage and combine with the other five Ms to most effectively grow and monetize your new business or offers?

Multipliers are marketing strategies and tactics. If you think about the first five Ms as ingredients to make a meal, then Multipliers are like a spice rack. They're how you turn up the heat (or flavor) on your Mindset, Market, Model, Messaging, and Media and create measurable outcomes.

Since the beginning of my career, I've developed, implemented, and earned hundreds of millions of dollars for myself and my clients as the result of approximately 30 different Multipliers — and I add more to the list regularly.

Multipliers are the battle plans where we execute. Not every Multiplier will work for every business or offer, and that's the fun part. When I'm working with my private clients, we spend most of our time hammering out the first five Ms, and then we finish up by creating a customized recipe with the Multipliers. When I work with clients in person, we spend our third day in the studio recording sales videos and webinars, working on pitch decks, and crafting magazine articles that get published in *Forbes*, *Entrepreneur,* and *Fast Company*. We get these done and published so quickly that clients are using them to close deals the same week.

Sometimes one Multiplier might be all that's needed, while for another client I'll recommend an assortment of a dozen or more. Don't get overwhelmed, though. The right Multipliers are the ones you're ready, willing, and able to put to work right away.

Here's a partial list of my best Multipliers:

- Referral Parties — $100k+ of New Business in Less than a Day
- The Ambassador Method — The Fastest Path to One-to-Many Buyers
- Money Phone — Close Deals Faster and Never Write a Proposal Again
- The Five Question Close — $25k-$500k Deals in One Conversation
- Bucket List Experience Multiplier — Turn an Experience into a Customer for Life
- Reactivation Machine — Turn Old Customers into New Buyers

Now that you have a working understanding of the six Ms, let's dive into each in detail.

CH. 2

MINDSET: HOW TO WIN AT BUSINESS AND LIFE

I have a condo that overlooks the ocean in La Jolla where I host business meetings and masterminds. When a client arrives for a three-day Superpower Accelerator workshop and sees the view, they reflexively breathe deeply, relax their shoulders, and issue a deep sigh as they gaze out over the deep blue Pacific Ocean. I start every day with them on the balcony, taking in the beach air, the sight of palm trees, and the sound of the waves crashing on the beach across the street. This is a reminder of what is important, eternal, and powerful.

There's something in us that knows success isn't about just the numbers in our bank account. Yes, money is a great scorecard, but if you're living a life that is out of alignment with your values, you're never going to be a success.

One question I always ask my Superpower Accelerator clients is, *"Are you willing to receive everything God and the universe has to offer and wants to give you?"*

Every Superpower Accelerator workshop is really about creating a new identity and installing an upgraded operating system with a founder. Learning how to receive is one of the hardest things for business owners to master. We're used to coming from nowhere, building our businesses with grit, resilience, and raw discipline. But at some point, our old operating system becomes obsolete. We've outgrown who we are, what we do, why we do it, and who we do it for. We need a reinvention to get to the next level.

> **Mindset is about congruence and alignment with who we are.**
> **It's also about attraction and repulsion.**

At our most fundamental, we are our values, what we're in favor of, and what we oppose. The strongest brands, businesses, and people have strong Mindsets and beliefs. They stand out against a society of people playing it safe, of those who refuse to take a stand, and of those whose opinions and positions flip-flop more often than a beached halibut. *When you don't know who you are and what you stand for, no one else does, either.*

Most people don't realize that most of their misery in business comes from not declaring and committing to their non-negotiable values. Whenever there's a discord between our beliefs/values and actions/agreements, we create clusters that are downright horrible to live through. That is why **effective strategies and tactics are always downstream from intelligent and accurate thinking.**

Your Mindset and values define your entire world, your company culture, and the employees and customers you attract.

One of the most useful tools I've used to clarify my values (and therefore the values of my perfect target Market), is *The Mindset Scorecard*. Full disclosure — thanks to my podcast partner, Dan Sullivan from Strategic Coach® for creating the scorecard model this version is based on.

THE MINDSET SCORECARD

Throughout my content (including in this book), you'll see a variety of scorecards I've created to help you define and measure different elements of your business. Don't skip these. I despise busy work and wouldn't have included them if they weren't important.

If you want to improve, you've got to measure — even something as abstract as Mindset. Measuring qualitative factors can be more difficult than tracking your quarterly P&L numbers, but it's just as critical.

In your Mindset scorecard, **you are defining the values or characteristics that are important to you. Then, you're** quantifying the degree to which you are achieving those values. The Mindset scorecard isn't just a navel-gazing exercise. What you define here will set the tone for the entire organization with regard to the culture you aspire to and your non-negotiables. Getting everyone on the same page is essential to organizational growth.

NOTE: I've included eight elements I've found to be invaluable in creating high-level business success. If one doesn't resonate with you, put on your big kid pants and change it up. Assessments and scorecards work best when they represent your values.

They also only work if you're honest. I know, you want to look good — but no one is looking at this but you. If you can't man- or woman-up and be straight with yourself, you've got issues beyond what I can help with in this book. If something is off in your life, admit it. Accept it. And then work your ass off to create a future where it's better.

1. TRANSFORMATIONS, NOT TRANSACTIONS

You know those people who call you out of the blue not because they want to check in on you, but only because they remembered you have season tickets to the Chargers and they're trying to score a pair for next week's game? Yeah, we all have been exposed to those transactional types who don't value you for you; they value you for the access or clout you can give them. People who view relationships only through a lens of exchange of favors are missing the big picture.

The Mindset Scorecard

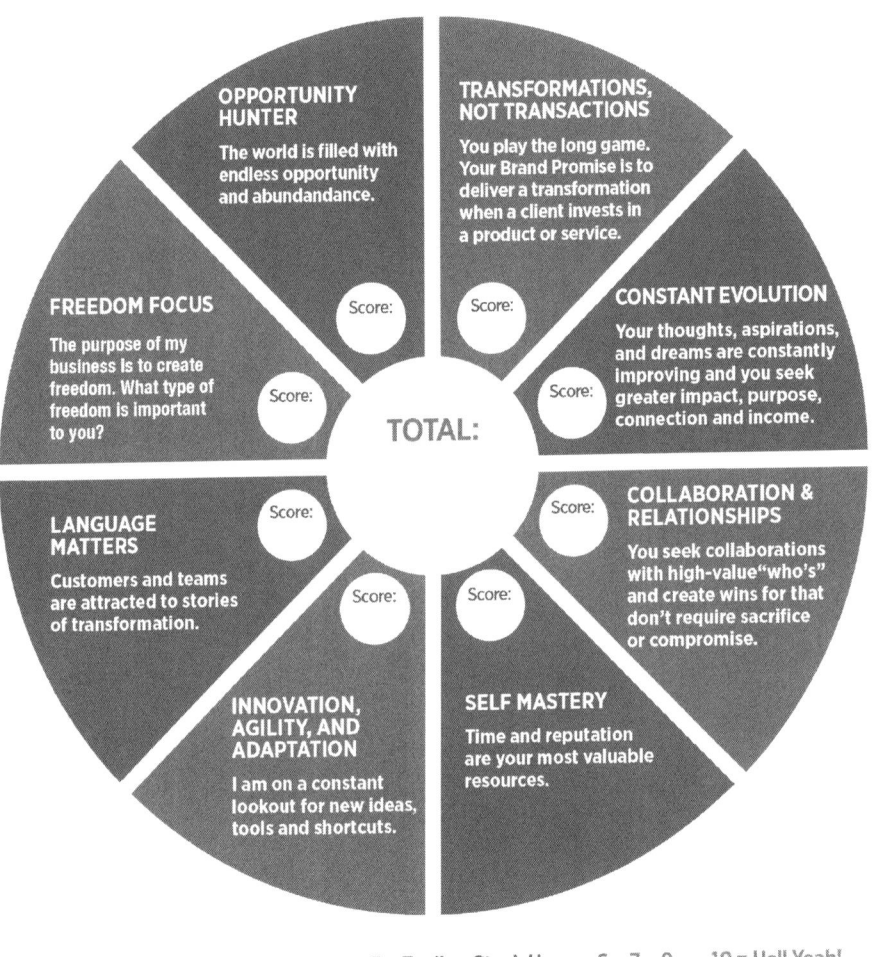

OPPORTUNITY HUNTER
The world is filled with endless opportunity and abundandance.

TRANSFORMATIONS, NOT TRANSACTIONS
You play the long game. Your Brand Promise is to deliver a transformation when a client invests in a product or service.

FREEDOM FOCUS
The purpose of my business is to create freedom. What type of freedom is important to you?

CONSTANT EVOLUTION
Your thoughts, aspirations, and dreams are constantly improving and you seek greater impact, purpose, connection and income.

LANGUAGE MATTERS
Customers and teams are attracted to stories of transformation.

COLLABORATION & RELATIONSHIPS
You seek collaborations with high-value "who's" and create wins for that don't require sacrifice or compromise.

INNOVATION, AGILITY, AND ADAPTATION
I am on a constant lookout for new ideas, tools and shortcuts.

SELF MASTERY
Time and reputation are your most valuable resources.

Score: (x8)

TOTAL:

1 = Can't even image that   2   3   4   5 = Feeling Stuck Here   6   7   8   10 = Hell Yeah!

- **0-45 =** You have a number of areas that may be out of alignment with your values, goals, and dreams. Pick one dimension to start, and commit to making changes.
- **46-65 =** You're generally moving in a positive direction but there are some areas that need to be addressed for greater momentum.
- **66-80 =** Your life is largely in alignment!

Mindset: How to Win at Business and Life

Unfortunately, many businesspeople see their customers not as individuals to be valued, but as walking bank accounts. Then they're surprised when there's no loyalty on the part of their clientele. That's because they've done nothing to earn that trust and loyalty.

That desire for transformation should reach beyond your business, too. Every relationship in your life, from your spouse to your kids to your friends, should be a place where you can mutually encourage each other to strive more, be more, and do more. You're constantly looking for a way to upgrade every part of your life, your body, your spirit, the quality of your relationships.

If people can't or won't grow and change for the better, you're willing to release them. You know you're here for something big, and that means in every area of your life.

2. CONSTANT EVOLUTION

Every living thing is dynamic. The cells in your body will completely renew and replace themselves every seven to ten years. Are your thoughts, aspirations, and dreams doing the same?

Let me put it this way. If I don't see you for a decade and when we get together you are exactly the same, there's something wrong— with *you*! I want to surround myself with people who are constantly evolving into new and better versions of themselves, who are operating more and more in their genius zones or, as I call it, their Superpowers.

Constant evolution means you're always looking for ways to experience freedom and expression. You're moving from:

- Human **DOING** (a minimum-wage burger flipper or "tasker") to
- Human **KNOWING** (valued for your knowledge. It's a step up from a "Doing," but it's white-collar wage slavery) to
- Human **BEING** (valued for who you are, what you know, and how you do it — an "influencer," category celebrity or thought-leader) to
- Human **EXPRESSION** (this is when you're living your true divine nature, transcending ego and old trauma.

The only thing limiting you from having or being anything you want is your identity, operating system, and willingness to let go of attachments, other's perceptions and judgments, and being willing to receive all the things God wants you to have)

I know, this can sound a little airy-fairy woo-woo, but even the greatest minds among us humans have seen the spark of the divine that lives in each of us. Carl Sagan said we're made of star-stuff. We're stardust, powered by starlight.

Do you find yourself drawn towards beauty and perfection? Are gratitude and love top of mind emotions for you? Then you can see the difference and feel the difference between low frequency and high frequency, and you eliminate low frequency, polarizing, negative people.

3. COLLABORATION & RELATIONSHIPS

This section takes the idea of transformation a step further. Scoring high means you understand great that collaboration creates exponential growth and that when the right people come together, 1 + 1 = 11.

Partnerships are important to you, particularly evolved partnerships where teamwork equates to greater productivity and efficiency. You know that working together allows you to go farther, faster.

When you value collaboration, you stop looking for 50-50 splits and seek opportunities to create full wins for all involved that don't require sacrifice and compromise.

Trust, obviously, is a key contributor to partnerships, and you trust others and yourself. You readily admit your own short-sightedness and weaknesses and partner with those who bring out the best in you by working within their own Superpowers.

4. SELF MASTERY

Are you constantly lashing out at anyone who attempts to provide guidelines or discipline — even if that means rebelling against yourself? If so, you may need to grow up and own your behavior. Leave the trauma-driven, self-pity, whiny toddler, victim mentality behind.

If you rate high in this area, you readily assume 100% responsibility for all your outcomes. You understand there are circumstances that are out of your control, yet whatever the situation is, you take complete ownership of it *as if* you are the person who caused it.

You're completely obsessed with creating new capabilities, gaining access to new tools, resources, people, and knowledge. You seek out mentors, and you have a history of investing in your growth and know the value of good advice. You probably belong to one or more business or coaching groups already because you know that belonging to a community of like-minded people rapidly accelerates your capabilities and holds you to a higher standard than you would hold yourself.

5. INNOVATION, AGILITY, & ADAPTATION

The older (and more devastatingly handsome) I get, the more I realize that the only thing life owes you is change.

There is not a single industry, technology, product, or service that is protected from disruption. From technological innovations (and subsequent obsolescence) to governmental regulations to worldwide pandemics, something will occur to throw a monkey wrench into your business plan. Tomorrow's profit is not guaranteed, and how you respond to that disruption will determine your level of future success. As a result, innovation, agility, and adaptation are three of the most powerful qualities we can possess as entrepreneurs. They allow us to play both offense and defense.

6. LANGUAGE MATTERS

Stories attract and repel, and that includes the stories you tell yourself. Humans are constantly seeking meaning, and since the beginning of time we've used stories to make sense of the world around us. When you embrace the power of language, you know your words and the stories you create matter greatly.

Scoring high in this category means you practice empathy and compassion in your words, and you adopt the language patterns of your client or prospect as a way to connect more directly with them and their values. You also know when (and how) to shut up and listen… valuing others' input as much as you do your own thoughts on a subject. You have trained yourself to think before you speak and to avoid pointless arguments. You recognize the power of language in all its forms, and you wield that power intentionally.

7. FREEDOM FOCUS

You're driven by freedom — of time, money, relationships, and purpose (what my friend, mentor, and podcast co-host Dan Sullivan of Strategic Coach calls "The Four Freedoms") — and realize that personal liberty is a higher value than pure monetary gain. You know that freedom is limitless, and everything you've experienced is only a fraction of what is possible. You actively seek to set yourself free from anything that controls you, your past, your addictions, or your limiting beliefs. You extract lessons from your past and then move on. You refuse to be trapped by anything or anyone.

8. OPPORTUNITY HUNTER

People who are opportunity hunters are always asking my favorite questions, *What if?... Imagine...* or *Let's try an experiment...* Great ideas, inventions, capabilities, and business are built with constant iteration. The world is one big sandbox, and you want to see what else you can build. Creativity and innovation — coupled with collaboration, of course — are your happy places. You don't unnecessarily limit yourself, but you also know that sometimes the most creative ideas come from constraints. You live in the land of possibility, not waiting for things to happen to you, but taking the reins to imagine a bigger, brighter, more powerful future. You can see it as clearly as the horizon in front of you. You are drawn by the lure of the future, knowing what value you can create for those around you.

■ ■ ■

Now that you understand each dimension, go through and rank yourself from 0-10. Find out where you are strong and where you are weak, and then decide what you're going to do about it.

WHAT LIFE DO YOU WANT *NOW*?

In Earl Nightingale's famous 30-minute recording, *The Strangest Secret*, he defined success as, "The progressive realization of a worthy ideal." It's an ongoing and progressive unfolding. The question becomes, *what life do you want **now**?*

How *big* do you think? What's the *scope* of your possibility for yourself and your business? If you didn't question or reject your potential, what would you choose to do, who would you choose to be, and what would you choose to have?

Ask yourself the following questions:

1. What do I really want to do?
2. Why do I do what I do?
3. What do I love?
4. What do I hate?
5. What do I fear?
6. Who do I trust?
7. Who do I admire?
8. How do I see myself?
9. How am I seen by others?
10. How do you want to be seen by others?
11. What do I want?
12. What do I believe?
13. What do I value?
14. How do my beliefs, values, and preferences match my business?

The *Dan Sullivan Question*®, a Strategic Coach® concept, is also one of the most funda-mental and useful mindset clarifying questions: "If you and I were to meet one to three years from today, what would have happened personally and professionally for you to feel happy with your progress?"

The Mindset section is all about making yourself the point of origin for your business. It's easy to get trapped in other people's expectations and agendas if you haven't defined what success, future, and accomplishment mean for you. By choosing what you want, what you value, and what you believe, you are able to create an orbit that attracts the right people. It also trickles into the model you utilize to make money, your Messaging, Media, and the Multipliers you will use to grow your business.

CH. 3

MARKET: CLAIMING YOUR TURF

IMPORTANT!

Many people are reluctant to even think about who they would love to work with because they think they can't have that. This is why it's critical to address Mindset before doing anything else. If you move into defining your Market and you are holding limiting beliefs about what you're capable of, what you "deserve," and what the Universe can bring to you, you're already starting off a foot race with your pants around your ankles. Make sure you spend time with the Mindset chapter before moving forward. I find that anytime I violate a Mindset non-negotiable, the result is frustration, aggravation, and chaos.

> **Never let the inmates run the asylum.**

Do you let your clients or customers bully you? No, really… this is a serious question. In fact, it's the very first question I ask when I start working with a new client. I want to know what percentage of their customer base is low frequency, meaning:

- They're bullies.
- They're abusive.
- They whine and complain.
- They're cheap, always angling for a deal.
- They play people against each other or threaten to escalate every interaction.
- Working with them is never clear-cut. It's always chaotic.

They occupy way too many of your waking hours, but when you even dare to think about cutting them loose, you quickly backtrack. "Well, they always pay on time…" "They've been with us forever…" and blah blah blah.

Sound familiar? If so, you are in good company. In my estimation, it's likely that a good portion (20 percent if you are "typical") of your current customers — possibly even the majority — fall into the "pain in the ass" category, meaning they are more trouble than they are worth. You make all sorts of justifications for keeping them around, but what it comes down to is that you're scared to fire them. They've got you whipped, and they know it. And despite your hopes that they'll improve, I guarantee you their attitude will go in only one way: Down.

Don't feel too bad if this hits a little too close to home. This situation is so common that it's one of the very first things we address when working with a founder.

With permission to be direct, I'll say, "Look, you've got a problem here. You need to earn the trust and respect of your team, and you need to do something drastic to do so. What I want you to do is to empower them. Give them the right and the responsibility to get rid of the bottom 20 percent of your clients who are probably causing 80 percent of the aggravation, damage, frustration, resentment, and anger inside of your organization."

When I say this, most people sit back like I've slapped them. They can't imagine cutting 20 percent of their client base. It immediately makes them think about a shrinking bank balance. But as we covered in the last section, there's more to life than money. No amount of money is worth being miserable.

And something else: The "hole" that opens up **will** be filled quickly with better clients, leading to growth in revenue AND happiness!

Let's do a little exercise right now. Imagine for a moment the top three customers or clients you've ever had, who you genuinely loved working with. It was easy to provide value to them, and you easily helped them implement and get significant results. They didn't complain. They didn't haggle over price. They didn't question your process or threaten your team members. These unicorns may only represent your top two percent, or even the top .2 percent, of people you've ever worked with.

Are Your Customers DREAMS or NIGHTMARES?

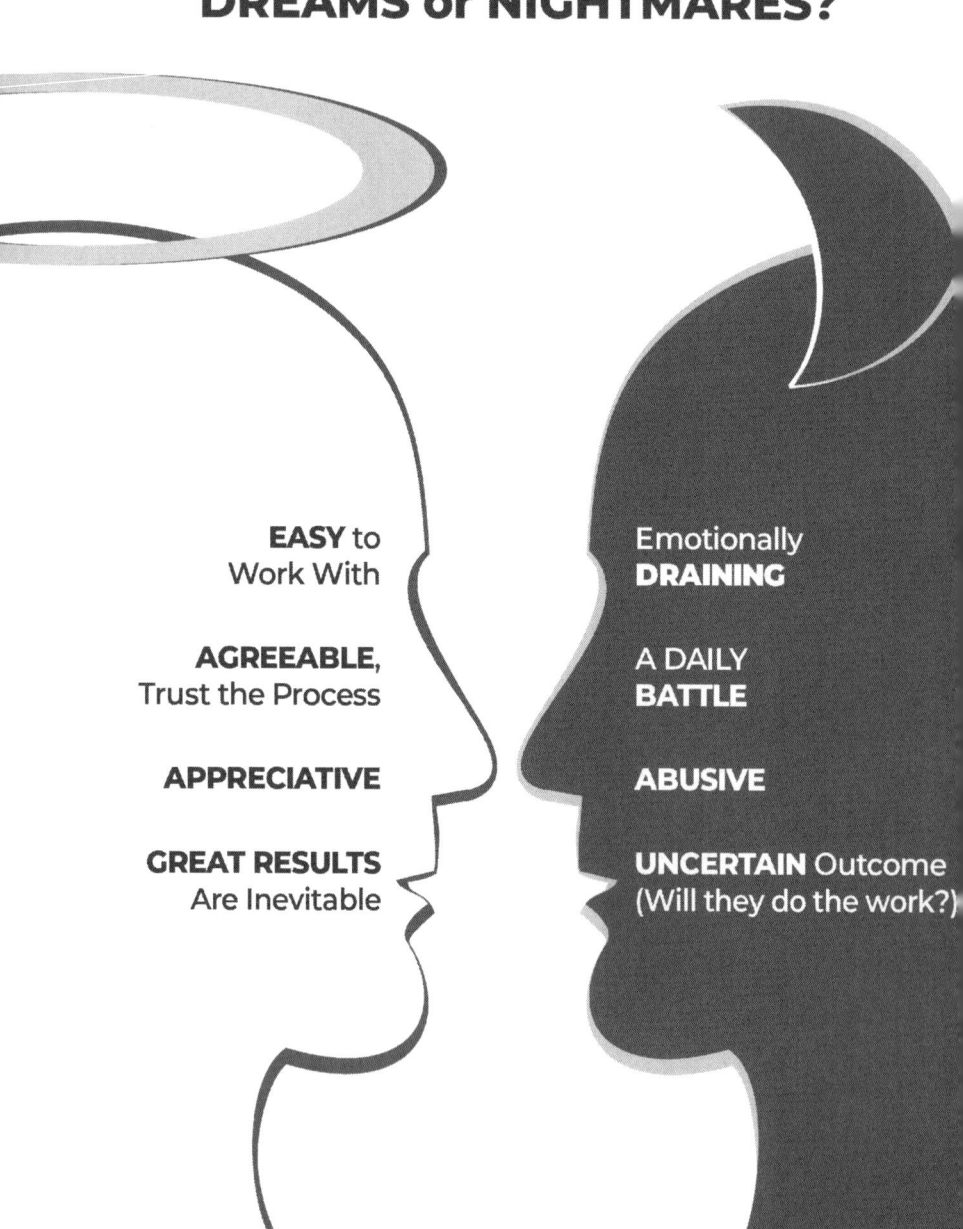

EASY to Work With	Emotionally **DRAINING**
AGREEABLE, Trust the Process	A DAILY **BATTLE**
APPRECIATIVE	**ABUSIVE**
GREAT RESULTS Are Inevitable	**UNCERTAIN** Outcome (Will they do the work?)

Can you imagine what your life would be like if your entire customer base was made up of clones of these customers? What if every minute of every day, you and your entire organization felt appreciated, effective, and well-compensated? How would that feel?

Now contrast that feeling with the nightmare customers I asked you about at the beginning of this chapter. I won't insult your intelligence and ask which you'd rather work with. We all know the answer.

You might be wondering why it matters so much that you like the people you serve. After all, money is money, right? Well, no.

The founders and business owners I work with tend to want meaning in their lives. They want to feel like what they do matters and, in Steve Jobs' words, puts a dent in the universe in some way. You can't do that if you're viewing what you do as a transaction with a nameless, faceless entity. Every interaction you have with someone takes something from you and gives something to you. Some may take joy and give frustration. Others may take stress and give pleasure. It's a transaction, sure, but it's a relationship first and foremost.

Here's a truth we don't always acknowledge: we have limited capacity. If your maximum customer base is, say, 100 units, there is a one-to-one relationship between these two groups. For every lousy, annoying customer you have, you're sacrificing working with an ideal customer. It's a zero-sum game. So if your business is 80 percent pain, misery, and chaos, you only have 20 percent available for happiness, joy, and abundance.

That's why your first move must be to fire the worst offenders to make room for your ideal clients.

In the rest of this chapter, we're going to clearly and precisely describe your perfect audience, or Market, in such a way that you immediately know if someone is a good fit, or if they're going to bring chaos.

> **IMPORTANT: You're a Business, Not a Charity**
>
> People who are broke or broken are NOT your problem. That is what charity is for. Those who serve the broke and broken will wind up broke and broken too. So if you feel moved to help those who are not in the mental, emotional, or financial space to work with you, allocate a percentage of your profit to charity. But don't make it part of your business to work with the broke and broken. If you do so, it will create absolute misery in your organization and sap the fun out of your work. Your business isn't a charity, but your business can support a charity. Do not confuse these two things.

YOUR PERFECT CLIENT

When we talk about your perfect client, we're looking at both demographics and psychographics. Demographics and psychographics are like two magnifying glasses that allow us to define a person's objective and subjective worlds.

Note that Mindsets and values precede demographics and psychographics.

Demographics refer to objective characteristics within a population. Demographics include things like:

- Education level
- Position or job title
- Age
- Income level
- Industry
- Gender
- Marital status

Psychographics can be difficult to measure. They include attitudes, aspirations, and other psychological criteria, such as:

- What's their perfect life?
- What prevents that from happening or being true?
- What opportunities do they wish they could take advantage of but can't for some reason?
- What are their Superpowers or zones of genius they want to express?
- Hobbies
- Values
- Personal profile — I particularly like the Kolbe assessment (www.MikeKoenigs.com/Kolbe), StrengthsFinder, PRINT, DISC, and Enneagram.

We're about to dig into three target Market exercises. All three use demographics and psychographics as their foundation. I suggest going through *all three* exercises as they each can shed additional light on your ideal client or customer. (Don't complain. It's good for you.)

THE 30-MINUTE AVATAR

Go back to the question I asked you earlier about your favorite customers or clients to work with. Bring one specific person to mind and answer the following questions:

What are their demographics?

What are their psychographics?

Write as many points as you can on 4x6 cards, with one point per card.

Then go back and repeat this process with a second member of your "favorite clients" group, and then a third and fourth, if possible.

After you have a stack of cards, look for similarities. Are they all in a certain industry? Do they all have a specific identifiable personality type? Are they all recently married or recently single? Do they share an affinity for long-distance running? Are they former athletes? Gather as much info as possible and create a single avatar with commonalities.

You can also do this with the customers who make you nuts. Involve your team. Have them fill out cards on the people who drive them crazy, getting as much detail as possible down. Then you'll be able to identify chaos the second it walks in the door.

YOUR PERFECT PROSPECT PROFILE

The 30-Minute Avatar exercise is good for quick wins. It's like a rough sketch or outline. I wouldn't base an entire new business model on it, but it can give some good insight and unveil some hidden patterns that you can use as a starting point. This next exercise is a much more detailed process. Your Perfect Prospect Profile is something you could use as a standard operating document for a brand vision.

The following document is excerpted from a strictly internal document. It's an abbreviated version of my own Perfect Prospect Profile that I'm sharing with you specifically because it's explicit and unapologetic.

You may read this and think it's a little obsessive, too specific, or over the top. But it's this level of detail and intention that enables us to attract the right people. This is the level of detail you need in your own Perfect Prospect Profile. You're instructing yourself: *"Here are the types of people I want you to be on the lookout for. Also, these are the types of people I want you to avoid like the plague."*

You will have different criteria for your target Market than we do. What you want is a picture so clear in your mind that you intuitively react to people when you meet them, listening for clues that tell you they're a *Hell, Yeah!* or *Hell, No!*

Title	- Business owner - Founder - Partner - CEO
Business	- B2B - $2 million - $250 million ++ - North America - 10-250 employees (unless they're a well-funded startup or experienced founder on 2nd-5th+ business) - Must have client transformations / social proof their products and services work - Must sell a product $10,000 or higher (ideally much more)
Personal Demographics	- 45+ - Male or female - $2 million+ net worth - $250k+ income (preferably $500k+) - Married (most likely with kids and pets) - English-Speaking (ideally in a US time zone). We do work with International Clients BUT they'll need to adjust for the 8am-6pm PST time zone.

Self-Identifiers	- Description on Twitter or LinkedIn includes:
	  ☐ Speaker
	  ☐ Author or Bestselling Author
	  ☐ Podcaster
	  ☐ TEDx or TED speaker
	  ☐ EO, YPO, Tiger 21 (or any of the belonger organizations)

Psycho-graphics	- Meditator
- Collaborator
- Paid for coaching in the past
- Interested in personal growth (e.g., Tony Robbins)
- Kolbe: "Quick Start" 8, 9, 10. Fast Decision-Makers
- Cause-oriented, give back, do philanthropic investments or work
- Libertarian-minded
- Spiritual / not religious
Avoid at All Costs	- FACT FINDERS — high KOLBE fact-finders are great team-members, but a pain as clients
- Fundamentalists
- Social Justice Warriors
- Blamers / Whiners
- Snowflakes / Victims
- "Alphabet Terrorists" and anyone associated with "cancel culture"
- Assholes
- Extremists
- Litigation attorneys or anyone with a history of litigation
- Only speakers, only coaches

Your Turn:

Here's a blank worksheet for you to describe your perfect prospect. You may want to make copies and hand them out to your trusted team members for their input.

Title	
Business	
Personal Demographics	
Self-Identifiers	

Psychographics	
Avoid at All Costs	

Market: Claiming Your Turf | 49

HOW TO READ MINDS

After speaking with hundreds of thousands of business owners, I have a more holistic view of those I can best serve, and those I most want to work with. There are certain things they say that make my ears stand up. I *know* I can help them by the way they talk about the pain they're experiencing. Once you've spoken with enough of your ideal clients, you'll also have this same sixth sense.

And once you master Messaging, you'll know exactly what to say to trigger their intrigue buttons so they want to become a client.

Here are the three main pain points I solve:

Category 1: Just Sold

"I just sold my business. Now what?"
What's going on in their head:

- "What I really want to do is…"
- "The reason I was doing what I was doing was so that I could…"
- "I have all the money I need. I want to create a bigger impact, create more purpose, and do something that's lifestyle compatible without so many moving parts."
- "I'm not ready to 'retire.' I have more in me for another act (or two!)."

- "I'm bored."
- "I'm ready for my Act 2, 3, 4, or 5… but I'm not sure what I should do next."

Category 2: Seeking to Maximize Revenue

"I know I'm leaving money on the table. I want to 10X my revenue so I can sell my products and services for a higher price to a better customer."
What's going on in their head:

- "How do I get my message out there?"
- "How do I go big and grow an audience?"
- "How do I monetize this vision beyond my company?"
- "We want to grow our business 10x or more."
- "We have great steak but lack sizzle."
- "We have a great product to sell but I know we aren't charging what it's worth and our messaging and positioning are off."
- "We are looking for ways to create MRR (Monthly Recurring Revenue) or turn our IP (Intellectual Property) into new products, services or passive income."

Category 3: Outgrown Current Business

"I've outgrown who I am, what I do, why I do it, and who I do it for."
"I'm stuck."
"I'm bored."

"I've forgotten how to think big or think outside the box."
"I'm depressed. Suicidal. I'm afraid to admit this to anyone around me because I don't want to scare them away or admit I don't have all the answers. I'm supposed to be the leader."
"I am pigeon-holed into category X when I'm capable of doing so much more."

What's going on in their head:

- "As a founder or CEO, I don't feel valued in my own organization."
- "I've evolved as a human being and want to express myself creatively and be valued for who I am versus what I do, know, or appear to be."
- "I want to grow this business and sell it so that I can…"

Now you have three strategies you can stack to help you define the perfect people you want to be a hero to.

Start with the simplest exercise: map out the demographics and psychographics of your favorite people. Add dimension to that exercise by creating your Perfect Prospect Profile. If you have the experience to amplify that profile, use the Pain Approach. Once you have a detailed description of your Market, you can use these assets in a number of ways, from onboarding team members to preparing marketing collateral.

Our next step is to figure out how you're gonna make some more cash.

CH. 4

MODEL: WHAT'S YOUR BRAND PROMISE?

What Transformation Do You Deliver, and How Do You Make Money?

When I talk about your Model, it is both the process you go through to provide results, as well as how you'll get paid for the transformation you provide your customers and clients.

One of the biggest mistakes business owners and founders make is confusing complexity with value. Having a 130-step process that takes months to implement may seem impressive to you, but what your customer really wants is results. They don't particularly care how you get there, as long as you have a process that works. Often, they'll pay extra for speed.

Think about going to two separate orthopedists because your knee is hurting.

The first one diagnoses your problem and says, "Here's what we're going to do. You're going to take the next three months and perform daily exercises that I lay out for you. They'll probably take about 30 minutes per day. At the end of three months, I'm going to fit you for a special brace that you'll wear 24 hours a day for the next six months. At the end of that time period, we'll see where you are. Chances are, you'll still need surgery, which will take about three months to get on my schedule for, and then a month or two to recover from. In just over a year, you'll be good as new!"

The second orthopedist diagnoses the same issue but says, "I have an opening in my surgery schedule tomorrow afternoon. We'll have you on crutches by this weekend, and back on the tennis court by the end of the month."

Which one would you choose? Which one would you pay more for?

People will pay a premium for simplicity and elegance. One time, I sat down at a mastermind event with a famous businessman I'd heard of, but never had the chance to meet. We were paired up for a partner exercise. I could see he was hurting, so we spent the entire hour on his situation. At the end of that time, I gave him a new, three-line business plan that would fit on a Post-It note, but that he was certain would bring him an additional $400 million in revenue.

Stop trying to make things complicated. More is not better, and fewer and simpler is not necessarily less.

When you consider your Model, think about transforming your products and services into an efficient, profit-producing system that facilitates all your goals and matches your values.

HOW TO MAKE MORE MONEY

There are really only three ways to grow any business. If you want to make more money in your business, you're going to have to figure out how to do one or more of the following:

1. Sell at higher prices
2. Increase the repetition and frequency of sales
3. Increase your number of customers

I've identified ten specific ways to achieve those outcomes. But before you dive into the following list, consider the most simple, direct route between you and more revenue: charging more for the products and services you already provide.

Don't skip this simply because it sounds too simple. It really is the "silver bullet" most business owners are looking for but are reluctant to implement for fear their customers will revolt. I'm not saying you should double your prices overnight, but… why not? It's going to be market- and client-dependent, but it's worth thinking about:

- How elastic or inelastic is the demand for your product or service?
- What ready substitutes do customers have?

- When was the last time you increased your prices?
- What is your margin now, and how does it compare to industry averages?

Start there, and then dive into the following ten paths for creating a more profitable business model.

1. Create a Larger Product Suite

Most businesses are very linear in their customer acquisition and service provision. They acquire a client or customer, sell a single product or service, and move on to the next customer. There's nothing inherently wrong with this approach, but it is very limited. It is a starting place, a foundation upon which to build.

In order to create an extraordinary Model, look for ways to expand that linear approach. Instead of serving a client once and seeing them to the door, look at where they've been, where they're going, and how else you might serve them.

I was talking with the owner of a publishing service who produces books for his clients, taking them from concept to published volume. He said he recently was kicking himself in the head because a former client of his had just dropped $1,000 with a competitor. Why? Because the client wanted to know how to create an audio version of her book — something he did not support.

"How long would it take you to walk your clients through the audio book process?" I asked him. The answer: a few hours.

"Is it something you can record a video course about, that they can then access on-demand?" The answer: yes.

10 WAYS TO PROFIT

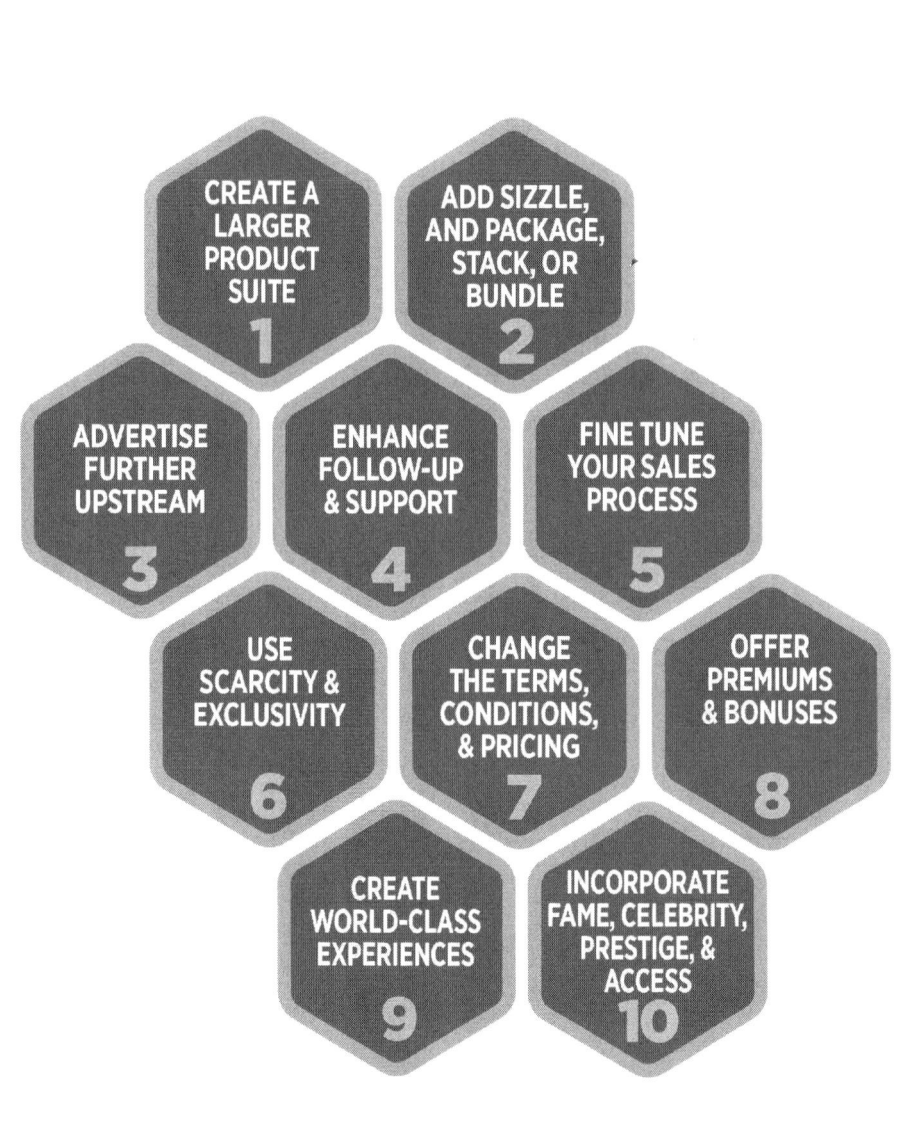

1. CREATE A LARGER PRODUCT SUITE
2. ADD SIZZLE, AND PACKAGE, STACK, OR BUNDLE
3. ADVERTISE FURTHER UPSTREAM
4. ENHANCE FOLLOW-UP & SUPPORT
5. FINE TUNE YOUR SALES PROCESS
6. USE SCARCITY & EXCLUSIVITY
7. CHANGE THE TERMS, CONDITIONS, & PRICING
8. OFFER PREMIUMS & BONUSES
9. CREATE WORLD-CLASS EXPERIENCES
10. INCORPORATE FAME, CELEBRITY, PRESTIGE, & ACCESS

"What percent of your clients want to create an audio book?" The answer: virtually all of them.

In a matter of hours, he could create an on-demand guide that would bring in a decent revenue stream. This was a no-brainer!

Ask what else your customer or client needs. What is the next step in their journey, and how can you serve them? Choose the easiest, most profitable options and add them to your Model.

2. Add Sizzle and Package, Stack, or Bundle

My client Joey Osborne says, "The fastest and highest ROI you'll ever get is to add more sizzle to your brand or offer. You can double or triple the value of your brand and equity value or increase the value of your offer 2X-10X by changing your story. Best of all, it can happen in days."

How you package your offer, the product stacks you create, and how you bundle products together impacts the perceived value, and therefore the price the client or customer is willing to pay.

Let's stick with the publishing example for now. The publisher has many small services he provides, including book cover design, copyediting, ghostwriting, and more. He also provides coaching and marketing support services, as well as lower-end DIY courses. How he packages his services, how bundles his products, and how he stacks them on each other as bonuses affects how much a client is willing to pay.

One "DIY" package might include all the on-demand courses plus access to a group for support as a bonus.

Another bare-bones package might be just publishing with no marketing or support services.

Then his high-end coaches might want an all-in-one premium package that includes everything from ghostwriting to full-service marketing.

The more exclusive and "done for you" a package appears, the more you can charge for it — provided the model meets your ideal Market's needs.

3. Advertise Further Upstream

If you own a home and are at the very early stages of considering selling, the first question you ask yourself is, "What's my house worth?" Knowing this, a real estate agent could advertise an annual house price guide for their geographic market. Because they're reaching the prospective client earlier in the selling process, they get a jump on all the other agents advertising to those clients who have already decided to sell and may already have an agent.

Marketing earlier in the process is a simple way to get more clients. You just have to know what question they are asking before you typically have your first contact with them.

4. Enhance Follow-Up & Support

Once you generate a prospect, how are you supporting them, answering questions, and leading them to the next step? One of my clients, Todd Brown, does a fantastic job of supporting his customers after they purchase a low-ticket offer. When you buy a copy of his book, he collects your phone number and email. When the book arrives, it comes with a letter to sign up for a free bonus membership (from which, of course, they're upsold into other products and services). Within a week of signing up, one of his team members calls you to hear a bit about your business and make sure you were able to access your bonus membership. This super-soft close works like crazy to bring people to the next step in Todd's funnel.

5. Fine-Tuning Your Sales Process

A good sales process is one that seamlessly moves a prospect from one stage of the sales cycle to another, as efficiently as possible, and has flexibility in pricing and perception. Strategic Coach has one of the most elegant sales processes I've seen. Their marketing team focuses on events that generate referrals and leads. They have appointment setters who fill the salespeople's calendars. Their salespeople have quotas. The whole process is fluid from beginning to end, with a focus on building a long-term relationship with the prospects, however long it takes them to become customers.

Application funnels are also a great way to establish authority with prospects. By asking the prospect to apply to work with you, you're exerting a subtle power play. Not only must they invest their time in filling out the application, you are also reserving the right to say yes or no.

6. Use Scarcity & Exclusivity

Legitimate scarcity and exclusivity work very well for services that offer high contact with you, such as coaching groups and masterminds. You can create desire and justify a higher price tag by limiting the number of enrollees, requiring a minimum income, or setting some other criterion. Done correctly, a program or product with scarcity and exclusivity becomes a badge of honor, one people will pay to access. A great example is the American Express Centurion Card, which has a $10,000 initiation fee and a $5,000 annual fee.

7. Change the Terms, Conditions, & Pricing

A few years ago I realized I wanted to sell my latest business and do something different. However, I didn't have a buyer. I did have about $1.5 million in fulfillment commitments and hotel contracts to fulfill. Shutting down the business was going to take 18 months and cost me $2 million to walk away.

Instead of biting the bullet and taking the financial hit, I created a business advisory program with $50,000, $75,000, and $125,000 price points. Most people would have set the agreements up for 12 months. Instead, I changed the offer. I said, "Most programs take 12 months. I'm going to deliver 12 months' worth of results in 6 months."

I filled that program, generated $2.5 million, and finished the fulfillment in 6 months with almost no overhead. That experiment became the basis of the business model I use to this day.

A real estate investor once told me that the listing price on a property was irrelevant. "I'm a cash flow investor," she said. "All I care about is the terms." What do your ideal clients care about? Are they more likely to go for a one-time fee or a subscription model? Do they want huge tax write-offs or smaller monthly invoices? One-time fees, monthly subscriptions, annual fees, installments, percentage of base… These are all ways to alter the perception of price.

8. Offer Premiums & Bonuses

Everyone likes a bonus; the cosmetics industry has made billions off the "free gift with purchase" model, with some people buying a product they don't really want, just to get a hold of the bonus. You can adapt this strategy to your advantage. Early in my career, I offered a course on how to create an information product using video. The bonus was a free Sony video camera. This was so popular that it led to my first back-of-the-room rush as people vied to make sure they received one of the limited number of cameras I'd brought with me.

If you offer a service, consider sending a direct mail package that includes a gift with high perceived value. It could be a quick-start guide, book, report, or ancillary support material that helps the person implement. Stand-alone coaching calls, live FAQ sessions, and tickets to a live event are all high-value ideas.

Whenever you are offering a premium or bonus, make sure it either answers an objection or you substantiate the value in a way that doesn't detract from the core offer. You don't want your premiums and bonuses to look like a bunch of junk you gathered off your hard drive and stuck on the website just for the sake of padding the offer.

9. Create World-Class Experiences

I used to hold mastermind meetings in hotels. Three meetings per year for $25,000. Boring.

I pushed "pause" on that business model for a few years until enough people asked me when I was going to start doing masterminds again. I asked myself, "What would make me super excited to do them again?" Answer: create bucket-list experiences that include a master wine sommelier, private chef, exotic locations, and content topics that I want to learn more about. I also wanted to do something that would excite my wife and the other spouses in attendance who can get bored at another basic business mastermind in a hotel.

Now I take my clients and their spouses to places like Guadalupe Valley, Baja Mexico. There are over 300 amazing wineries there. We travel with a master sommelier and private celebrity chef and eat like kings and queens. We stay in exclusive locations that require you "know a guy" to get into. Our topics include life extension (including full body and brain scans), cryptocurrency investing, and artificial intelligence hedge funds. I make sure our agenda provides lots of time for connecting and relationship-building.

Best of all — spouses ask members, "When's the next mastermind?!"

Want to create an irresistible offer? Consider the setting. The more memorable it is, the harder it will be for anyone else to replicate your offer.

10. Incorporate Fame, Celebrity, Prestige, & Access

99.9 percent of businesses are replicable, especially those doing less than $10 million in revenue. The main difference between one business and another is not objective. It's perception. It's the feeling a person gets when they buy. That's why fame, celebrity, prestige, and access are all important enhancements to your Model. What kind of access can you provide your clients that they cannot get elsewhere? For instance, one of the Multipliers we offer our clients is featuring them in an article that is placed in *Fortune, Fast Company, Forbes*, or *Entrepreneur*. This is access to showing up in print that they likely can't get elsewhere, and it contributes to their fame, celebrity, and prestige. They're willing to pay a premium for the perceived value.

I introduce and connect my clients to celebrity connections and friends, including bringing them with me when I attend invite-only concerts or meetings.

The Trifecta: Get Paid, Get Laid, & Live Forever

Excuse the crassness, but the phrase is memorable. From a consumer's emotional point of view, they'll trade their hard-earned money for these three main promises. Whether they're buying a laptop, a vacation, or a coaching program, all products and services fit into one of only three categories. They want to get paid (more money), get laid (increase their status, authority, brand, or thought leadership), or live forever (improve their lifestyle, lifespan, or healthspan).

People will buy from you in order to make more money. I call it "selling money at a discount." One of my brand promises is that you'll get your original investment after working with me in less than 60 days. One of my recent clients, Michael Chu, spent three days with me for a Superpower Accelerator workshop and within two weeks closed $1.2 million.

Next is status. The clothing and accessories we wear, the people we associate ourselves with, the car we drive, the home environment we live in — all may raise our status relative to those around us. This can also include becoming a bestselling author, getting publicity, raising public awareness, creating a consumer brand, or anything that positions you as an authority, thought leader, or expert. We want to be followed, admired, and respected. When you can provide that to your clients, it translates into being able to dramatically increase your prices.

People will also pay for health or lifestyle. Everyone wants to live longer, live better, live healthier. They want endless sex drive and youth.

When you create or improve your business Model, make sure you're baking in at least one of these elements and making it clear that it's part of the transformation you provide. To increase your perceived value, increase the certainty with which they'll achieve their goals.

In this section, we covered the three ways you can make more money with your Model: by increasing your prices, your frequency of sales, and the number of customers. A linear business Model is just the beginning; review this chapter and choose at least one specific way to amplify your Model.

Up next, we'll master your Messaging through a series of distinctions that will help you articulate your message in a way that captures the mind and heart of your ideal prospects and compels them to take action.

CH. 5

MESSAGE: TELL A POWERFUL STORY

"Once upon a time there was someone just like you... who tried and failed to get results. You met a guide who gave you insights, shortcuts, capabilities, and resources to slay the dragon, rescue the princess (or get the prince), find the Holy Grail, and live happily ever after."

This is "The Hero's Journey" or monomyth. It's the foundation of every religion, movie, story, and even great song. The *Star Wars* saga follows the formula perfectly. So does Dorothy's journey in *The Wizard of Oz,* as well as just about every Disney movie, from *Finding Nemo* to *The Incredibles.* We are fundamentally wired to respond to stories of struggle and redemption. It's how information and ideas have been transferred for millennia.

As I was thinking about my years of experience with copywriting, messaging, and brand-building, I asked myself, "What is the most fundamental messaging strategy or tactic a business owner should understand above all others?" Hands down, it's mastering the art of storytelling. Joseph Campbell's "Hero with a Thousand Faces," "The Hero's Journey," and "The Power of Myth" have driven many scriptwriters to success, including George Lucas.

Creating a winning Message is all about telling strong stories that break through the trust barriers and rapidly convert right-fit prospects into paying customers. Your goal is to help your prospects see themselves in a movie with them in the leading role.

Here's a more detailed example of the story.

Once upon a time, a lonely hero was trying to find a solution to a difficult challenge. A sudden and unexpected journey promised an adventure. Peril appeared. A princess/prince needed help and a dragon stood in the way of our hero's mission. It tested our hero's character, strength, and skill.

After trying and failing again and again, the hero was visited by someone who appeared from the smoke-filled background: a mentor / Yoda / Glinda the Good Witch / Jesus / Buddha who holds all the secrets. The mentor teaches our hero the way of the forest. He provides a sword, a couple of magic spells, the talisman, and a magic wand for good measure. (Assets, baby!)

But first, our hero must overcome past trauma, fears, and beliefs that hold him back from being a true hero and attractive to the one they seek… Wax on, wax off, destroy that old ego and identity.

Finally, our hero has the tools, mindsets, and power he or she needs to kick some dragon ass. Our hero is pumped up, ready to rock 'n' roll!

BAM! POW! ZANG! KABOOM! The dragon is dead! Our hero is alive. The hero picks up the princess/prince and they kiss as the sun sets behind them and a flock of doves flutter down and rest ribbons, rose laurels, and coins of gold upon their feet.

… and the whole scene gets transformed into an emblem that a biker gets tattooed on his chest!

Done correctly, Messaging is the perfect magic button. It pre-sells your prospects, answering the questions:

- Who are you?
- Why should I trust you?
- Why should I care about what you are selling?
- What are you going to do for me?

In the fewest number of words, you will grab your ideal prospect's attention, build trust, create credibility, and influence them. The result? They raise their hand and say, "Hey! You understand me. It's like you're reading my mind. How do we start working together?"

What Good Messaging Accomplishes

There are a million and one different books, courses, and ideas about the "right" way to create copy and Messaging. Many are

The Hero's Journey:
Superpower Accelerator Version

Once upon a time…

A hero encounters a "dragon" and is called to an adventure…

After many failures, he meets a magical mentor…

Who helps him conquer his past demons and overcome his doubts and fears…

And vanquish the dragon…

And re-emerge, victorious, and **REINVENTED!**

a waste of time. Some actually work. At the root, here's what your Messaging must do for your ideal client:

1. **Capture their attention with a novel hook.** A hook grabs someone's attention. It interrupts the "mindless scroll" on social media, stops them in their tracks if it's a billboard, brings them back from the kitchen or bathroom if it's a TV commercial. It's something that breaks through and says, "Stop! This is interesting!"
2. **Establish credibility.** There are many ways to create trust. Images of you with famous people. Transformations. Success stories. Proof of past experience. Testimonials of previous clients. All of these establish the fact that you have helped other people — people who are just like your prospect.
3. **Make a massive promise.** Identifying your prospect's problem and pain isn't enough. They need to know you can actually solve that problem. You must ask for the sale by making a massive promise. It tells people what to expect, and it reassures them that you are going to deliver something they value.

Put these three elements together with the proper Mindset and Model for your ideal Market, and you'll have a hell of a pitch.

Here's an example of a winning pitch, one of the fastest closes I've ever experienced. See if you can identify the three elements mentioned above.

I was attending a large event when a guy walked up to me. "Hey, I'm Charlie Epstein." Charlie, who was in his 60s and looked a bit like Larry David, said he was a financial advisor, and I had to force myself not to flee immediately. After all, financial advisors are not always known for scintillating conversation. Still, Charlie was a pretty interesting guy. It turned out he'd been following me for a while, was bored, and wanted something new, something different, something that offered more than just financial rewards.

He went on to say that he was known as America's 401(k) Coach. (*"Kill me now,"* I *was silently screaming. "How long before I can duck out?!"*)

But something about him grabbed me. After a little probing, I discovered he had once done stand-up comedy, theater, and television (including *Guiding Light*), was a busker and played guitar and sang in London's Underground. (*"I may be able to work with this," I thought…*) I told Charlie to give me a bit of time to make a few calls.

I called a former employee, now a professional comedian. "Hey Kyle," I greeted him, "How'd you like to work with me in putting together a comedy show for a financial advisor?"

He thought I was joking. After I convinced him I was serious, I told him I wanted to find a few other full-time career comedians who had also written for TV. Kyle was intrigued by the challenge and lined up a couple of guys to be our writing team.

I went back to Larry David, I mean Charlie, and said, "Charlie, here's the deal. You have one minute to make up your mind. I put together a team of professional comedians to write a one-man show about your life, your business, and the myths of money. You in?"

It didn't take him more than a second before he said, "Stop right there. I'm in. Where do I wire the money?"

Signed, sealed, and a few weeks later, we delivered "Yield of Dreams." We all got together and outlined and created a one-man show for Charlie in two days. That one-man show was featured in an article and video for *Entrepreneur*, and became an app, a product, a documentary, a series of animations, and even an interactive game. Right now, Charlie is shopping a television version of the program.

With two showings of the play, Charlie generated over $1.2 million in new business over a span of two months, beating what top performers in his business might do in a year.

Do you see why this worked so well? Charlie got what he wanted — even more than he *thought* he wanted. I was able to quickly identify his pressing pain points and create a memorable offer, complete with a massive promise. And then my team and I more than delivered on it.

Now, Charlie keeps coming back for more because every time we work together, he receives a transformational experience.

I was able to do this because first of all, I had the right Mindset. I knew that I could create a complete transformation for my ideal client. And because I was so clear on who I do and do not work with, I was able to quickly decide whether or not Charlie Epstein fell into that ideal Mindset and Market category. Once I knew he was a good fit, I offered him a Model that promised transformation, and I put it all together in a powerful Message that put him in the starring role.

When I put Messaging together for Charlie, I was thinking of him and only him. I knew that if he was in my .2 percent of top clients, the pitch would resonate. I knew exactly what my Model was, and the results, outcomes, and benefits he'd realize. By the time I presented it to him, it was a done deal. He would have been crazy to say no to something that addressed the exact pains he was feeling and promised to alleviate the source of those pains in a matter of days.

I created a future for Charlie that he could easily see and step into — but one he could not achieve on his own. He could envision himself on the stage with my help, not just as America's 401(k) Coach, but as a star.

The One-Word Pitch

I asked Dan Sullivan, founder of Strategic Coach and my podcast partner, "What's the best pitch you've ever heard?" Dan went on to tell me his favorite pitch… actually a one-word offer that Julius Caesar made to a belligerent band of soldiers, comprising men who were conquered subjects of Rome.

At the time, tensions were high as the army was protesting poor treatment and was on the verge of revolting and waging war against the Romans. Things could have gotten ugly, but Caesar knew what these men wanted. He knew their pain. He knew what they needed in order to calm down. In a single word, he offered it to them: *Civitatis*, meaning citizen. He offered them the citizenship they wanted, if they laid down their arms and did not continue with the uprising. The army responded, and peace was restored.

The key to this story is how well Caesar knew his audience. He had the proper Mindset and the right Model (citizenship). And so all it took was a one word Message to close them.

One-word offers aren't just the product of history books. There are many brands that are so clear in what they offer, that their mere name holds the massive promise. Coca-Cola. Apple. Porsche. These brands are pre-framed, so the offer is clear. Attention, trust, influence, emotion… it all exists in a single word.

What word would immediately resonate with your ideal Market? Freedom? Security? Sex? Attention? Bliss? Spend some time thinking about it. What would you need to do to pre-frame your offer so just that one word would be enough to frame a close?

The One-Minute Pitch

Okay, a one-word pitch is almost impossible by itself without proper framing. Let's be a little more reasonable. I'll give you a full 60 seconds. If you had just ONE MINUTE to pitch your product, service, company, or yourself to your perfect client, what would you say? What would make them beg to work with you, buy your product, or invest in your business?

Recently, I had the incredible opportunity to be on *Elevator Pitch* with Entrepreneur.com. It's sort of like "Shark Tank" with a stricter time limit. I listened to a ton of pitches (both good and bad), but I was completely blind to the people pitching as well as to the other judges. The judges could either cut deals together or screw each other over, and it got pretty crazy.

The whole experience brought up a burning question: What makes for a really great pitch?

One of the most important elements is this: *Tell authentic stories.* It starts by being able to tell stories that engage the audience's intellect and emotions. Share your vision, goals, and stories of hope, inspiration, motivation, transformation, and transcendence. When you tell your true, raw, uncut and authentic story, people will trust you, believe you, and magical things will happen in your business.

What really grabs an audience is your "why" — WHY are you doing what you're doing? My client Steve Marler, who runs AdvancedBodyScan.com, tells a story about how his mom died a painful death from breast cancer. It could have been prevented if the doctors had discovered and diagnosed her sooner. He started a scanning company that can do a full body scan in four minutes without injections, needles, dyes, contrasts, or anesthesia and with minimal radiation exposure. 11 years and 65,000 scans later, he's saved thousands of lives with early detection — including his 94-year-old father. Steve was able to discover not only a major heart issue, but also cancer. With early detection, the issues were addressed and Steve has been able to enjoy his dad for an extra 10 years.

Steve knows first-hand that early detection saves lives.

Steve is naturally a good storyteller, but after I worked with him to tell a short *why* story every time he described the business whenever he goes on TV, his leads jumped two to three times what they'd been previously. People trust people and brands when they understand *why* they do what they do. It fills in the gaps and holes of distrust and cynicism.

Steve's story is simple:

- His mom died a slow painful death.
- It could have been prevented with a scan.
- Early detection saves lives.
- He saved his dad's life twice.
- Early detection saves lives — what if you could have been with a loved one an extra month or ten years?
- The health care system is a broken sick-care system — our treatments and doctors are great, but we catch problems after it's too late and play whack-a-mole instead of preventing the disease from becoming a problem in the first place.
- Steve is on a mission to save lives.

What kind of story can you tell about your business, your brand, your transformation in just 60 seconds that outlines your big "why" and what you believe??

Create Your Hero's Journey

Test the following out for yourself. I promise it's going to blow your mind. Take out your phone or some sort of recording device, hit record, and speak the following story template out loud. Just fill in the blanks. Don't worry about whether you screw up. If you make a mistake, try it again on the same recording. It's one thread; one stream of consciousness that you create, without editing yourself. Just speak the words as they come out.

Your Perfect Prospect is the star of the following movie:

_____ embarked on a journey to solve
         Name

_____ .
                  problem

1. Along the way, _____
                              Name

   encounters a series of roadblocks including…

   _____ ,
                 points of conflict

   _____ ,
                 trials and errors

   _____ ,
                 a competitor

   _____ .
                 misdirection, etc.

2. Thankfully, _____ discovers
                          Name

   _____ .
                 your solution

   Skeptical at first, _____ feels
                                Name

   _____ .
               hesitations/objections

Yet, _____ considered the
          Name

_____ .
                  alternatives

3. _____ implements the solution.
            Name

   a. (Lay out the exact process)

      i. First… _____

      ii. Then… _____

      iii. Finally… _____

   b. Within _____ , _____
                   time   Name

     started seeing results such as _____
                                        name results

_____ .

4. Finally, _____ solved the problem.
                 Name

   a. Looking back, _____ was
                              Name

   _____ and now _____
       summarize past, include emotions   Name

   is _____ .
           summarize current, include emotions

Message: Tell a Powerful Story | 79

Speak that story out loud at least five times in a row. Meaning, repeat the same story of that perfect prospect over and over again, at least five times. Notice how each time you speak it, you clarify your points, and refine the story into something that's more summarized or "tight."

The following is a direct voice-to-text note of me speaking a client success story into this book using the above template. I only edited a few words that came out incorrectly. It may not follow the above process in exact word-for-word detail. The point is getting the draft done. Check it out…

Charlie Epstein went on a journey to solve a problem: people suffer money problems because they believe in myths about money that aren't true. He's a financial advisor who sells "me too" products and needs to stand out from the crowd.

He had joined "all" the masterminds, wrote a book, and created a tremendous amount of marketing material and was making good money. Yet, something was missing. He wanted to develop something that would engage his Unique Abilities® as an actor, comedian, and entertainer at a new level.

He discovered the Superpower Accelerator. Skeptical at first, Charlie didn't know if it would work for him because he had tested so many different things.

Charlie went to San Diego, worked with me and the Superpower Accelerator team. Charlie, me, and a team of writers produced a business comedy in a television writer's room environment, building a one-man comedy show based on Charlie's life called "Yield of Dreams — Paychecks for life."

Finally, he had the asset that fueled his regular and ordinary business into a new expression of passion and potential.

In addition to the show, Charlie's podcast, offer, App, documentary, and articles on Entrepreneur.com provide additional proof and credibility. Looking back, Charlie was bored and wondering what his next level was. Now, he's reinvigorated, amped up for the future, and making 10X Multiplier moves!

Is that perfect? No. It isn't. I took my best shot using the template to communicate a real client success story. Does it tell a reasonable beginning, middle, and end that makes sense? Yes. It does. That is all we are looking for. It's getting it out of your head – not getting it "perfect."

Powerful Messaging takes some practice, tweaking, and experimentation. Often, you won't know how something will work until you try it out. That's why I want you to get started with this now. Whether it's the One-Word Offer, One-Minute Pitch, or Hero's Journey, get something down and try it out. Once you get a workable message, try it out on some real prospects. Then you can move on to the next accelerator, Media.

CH. 6

MEDIA: FISH WHERE THE FISH ARE BITING

Media has gotten a bit of a bad reputation lately. Much of it has turned into polarized, politicized, untrustworthy crap. Social media companies are viewed as hostile to certain perspectives. Americans' trust in the media has cratered in recent years. But that doesn't mean Media doesn't work. We're all consuming Media every day in some format. Where do your perfect customers consume their information? What format do they trust?

POPULAR MEDIA FORMATS

- TV
- Radio
- Newspapers
- Magazines
- Podcasts
- Books (audio, print, or electronic)
- Live events
- Online events
- Direct mail
- Email
- Mobile text
- Telephone
- YouTube
- Instagram
- Facebook
- LinkedIn
- Telegram
- Twitter
- TikTok
- Snapchat
- Clubhouse
- …and new ones as they emerge

You need to determine where your Messaging needs to live to reach the maximum number of your perfect prospects and clients. What is the most effective "recipe" of different formats and channels to increase awareness, share your transformation stories, and convert prospects to customers?

Fighting Media Overwhelm

The average human attention span is now shorter than a goldfish's (which, by the way, is only nine seconds). They've got us beat by a second — and ours is dropping rapidly, down to eight seconds from 12 seconds in 2000.

- Website page views lasts an average of only 10 – 20 seconds
- Users read 20 – 28 percent of the words on a webpage, blog, or article
- An average person picks up their phone 344 times per day — every four minutes

That's just the start of it. Aside from the number of distractions, the frequency of exposure has increased significantly, too. Americans are exposed to an estimated 4,000 to 10,000 ads *per day*. (Most of them suck, by the way.)

It's a thumb-flick, swipe right world. So instead of just complaining about it, what are you going to do about it?

It all comes down to knowing your Market and developing Messages that instantly connect with them in the Media they most rely upon, trust, and enjoy.

Here are some tips for fully utilizing your chosen channels.

13 Laws of Media

1. **Focus on one channel at a time.** It's tempting to try to increase your media presence in one big leap but trying to do

too much at once is a recipe for frustration. Don't spread yourself too thin with your Media production. Treat different forms of Media like the plates spun on sticks by circus performers. Focus on one plate first. Once you get it spinning, then you can add the next, and the next, and the next. Make sure you have a workable strategy for each channel before you add another.

2. **Never fall in love with a Media channel.** Just because a channel exists does not mean you need to use it. Don't listen to the "gurus" who say you HAVE to be on TikTok or Twitter. Not every platform works for every business or every business owner. Do what works – nothing more, nothing less. I've met plenty of people who think they have to have a podcast or a vlog or a book or whatever… but their ideal client isn't anywhere near that channel. For instance, there are a lot of businesses out there wasting a ton of time trying to "go viral" on TikTok when their ideal client doesn't even know what TikTok is. If a channel isn't connecting you with the perfect person, dump it like a bad date.

3. **Choose which medium you work best in.** Not everyone was meant to be on video or to write a book or to host a daily call-in podcast or radio show. Written word, audio, and video: Which one do you work best in? My friend Robert G. Allen puts it this way, "Are you a speaker who writes, or a writer who speaks?" Take the easy route to content creation. I'll sit down and think using just a pen

13 Laws of Media

1. Focus on one channel at a time.
2. Never fall in love with a media channel.
3. Choose which medium you work best in.
4. Engage with the right people.
5. Play the long game.
6. Execute imperfectly.
7. Do not compare yourself with anyone else.
8. Repurpose and repackage wherever possible.
9. Share the heavy lifting with complementary/non-competing businesses.
10. Go for value.
11. Understand and model the greats.
12. Be a relentless student of direct-response.
13. You're an attention-getting entertainer.

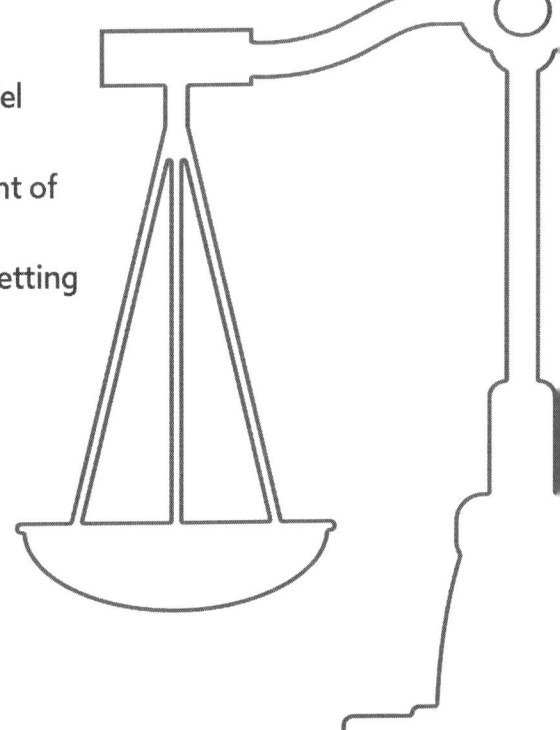

and paper, then picture-to-text it into Google docs. Other times, I'll record an idea right into an AI transcription service. Other times it's a video to a VA who will transcribe for me. Use whatever increases the likelihood that you will actually create something.

4. **Engage with the right people.** The purpose of Media is to increase engagement with your ideal Market. It's easy to fall into the trap of vanity metrics, getting fooled into believing your marketing is working based only on the number of followers you have on various platforms. Remember, it doesn't matter if you have a blue checkmark and a Twitter following of 100,000 if none of them will ever buy from you. Keep your eyes on the prize.

5. **Play the long game.** Developing content is both a sprint and a marathon. You must do it daily, but it can take an extended period of time until you see the results. Before you get started, commit to the long haul. Don't judge the success or failure of your efforts in the short-term. Plan on waiting at least 90 days to measure impact.

6. **Execute imperfectly.** Don't overthink about getting everything in order before you start producing. You'll never think you're ready. Instead, jump in and adjust along the way. If I had waited until I knew what I was doing before recording my first podcast, writing my first book, or recording my first video, I never would have started! You'll only be able to improve if you take that first step. Start earlier,

fail fast, fail forward, and keep trying. Experimentation is encouraged. Imperfect and published is better than perfect and unpublished.

7. **Do not compare yourself with anyone else.** It's easy to look at an Instagram influencer or YouTube personality with millions of followers or subscribers and get discouraged. But all of us — even the "big guns" — started at zero. If you ever find yourself falling into that comparison trap, always take note of how far you've come. Compare your current progress only to where you've come from, not to where you're going or expect you should be (or where anyone else is).

8. **Repurpose and repackage wherever possible.** My motto is: create once, use 100 times. Whether it's turning blog articles into a downloadable report, a book into an audiobook, or a series of videos into a course, seek new ways to repurpose and repackage your material. I create my content once, then distribute it in multiple formats. I call this multicasting. For instance, these words you're reading now are ones I dictated and transcribed. I start with a bullet list of ideas I want to cover, speak my thoughts into my phone, and then pass it on to an editor to clean it up and make it print-ready. Always be thinking about how else you can reuse your content.

> **Multicasting: Creating content once and distributing in many different forms.**

9. **Share the heavy lifting with complementary/non-competing businesses.** During a recent Superpower Accelerator session, I shared an idea with Steven Marler for easily producing content for a book he wants to create to promote his Advanced Body Scan business. He was committed to writing a book, but wasn't sure he had the time, content, or stamina to do it himself. I suggested that Steven get five of his most trusted vendors or partners to contribute a chapter or two to his book. Not only does it make content creation easier, but it also gives the contributors a vested interest in making sure the book is a success. They'll gladly promote something they helped create.

10. **Go for value.** Want to make sure the content you create has the best chance of landing with your target audience? Stop thinking about "marketing" and start thinking about "value." Load your material with valuable insights people can use, in a format they can easily access and digest. This does two things. First, it creates genuine good will in the marketplace. Second, it removes the burden to "perform." When your focus is on the end-user, the rest takes care of itself.

11. **Understand and model the greats.** The best advertisers throughout history — people like David Ogilvy, Dan Kennedy, Claude Hopkins, John Caples, Jeff Walker, Eugene Schwartz, John Carlton, Frank Kern, Joe Sugarman, and Gary Halbert, to name a few — have been responsible for breakthrough advertising promotions that captured the imagination of the masses and compelled them to buy.

If you're serious about becoming a better marketer, create your own swipe file of ads and frameworks. While Media channels may have changed, basic human psychology has not. Don't be a dick, though. You're not copying their material and distributing it as your own; you're using their work as a launchpad.

12. **Be a relentless student of direct-response.** It's ironic when I hear business owners complain about getting bombarded with advertisements on various Media channels. Instead of complaining, they should be paying attention. If an ad is popping up again and again, it's because it's working. Use it to inform your own efforts. Click over to the next page. Sign up. Buy. See what other people are using to convert prospects to their offer. You never know when you're going to stumble upon a great copywriting or marketing idea.

13. **You're an attention-getting entertainer.** Years ago, I worked with Tony Robbins and helped him create some products and marketing campaigns. I spent a day with him at his house, and when we were done for the day, he pulled me aside and said something that horrified and angered me at the same time. "Mike, I'm an entertainer. 80 percent of what I do is entertainment, 20 percent is content. But if I don't entertain, nobody will pay attention, and we won't produce the transformations we do." I wanted to scream. Just hearing that blew up the illusion of who I thought Tony was. But he was right then and even more today. Before you can get paid to do what you do, you have to:

- get attention;
- gain trust;
- establish thought leadership, status, and authority; and then
- convert a reader/listener/viewer/attendee/referral into a buyer. If you don't have all the customers you want, you talk too much, teach too much, and aren't good at one or all of the above.

Putting It All Together

A real-life example of what we did with our client Justin Donald can help you see how all the pieces come together. When I met Justin, he had a Unique Ability® to invest money and generate passive income and cash flow from that to cover his total net expenses. Unfortunately, he was flying under the radar. He knew there were tons of people out there who could benefit from his expertise, but he had no idea how to reach them or in what format. After a few conversations, Justin said he wanted to work with me for a Superpower Accelerator workshop in order to figure out how to get more visibility (and money) for his work.

It was easy for me to see the potential. He wasn't just another investment wiz; he was a master of producing passive income! After going through Mindset, Market, Model, and Message, we started talking about what Media would best support his business. We decided on a combination of magazine articles, followed by a book that we'd take to best-seller status.

I wrote an article about Justin, who I called the investment world's new Warren Buffet. I placed the interview in *Entrepreneur* magazine, which rapidly positioned Justin at the top of Google for his SEO results. In addition, during his Superpower Accelerator workshop we created the 10 Commandments of Lifestyle Investing, which later evolved into the subtitle of his book.

I also wrote a second article, which we published in *Forbes*: "The Four Core Principles of Lifestyle Investing." (Note: this is a great example of multicasting. We took a new spin on the same basic content and placed it in a different magazine). Then Justin wrote *The Lifestyle Investor: The 10 Commandments of Cash Flow Investing for Passive Income and Financial Freedom*, which is available as a hard cover, Kindle book, paperback, and audio book (we've learned over time that different formats attract and communicate with different audiences). Now here's the great news: Justin's book reached #1 on the *Wall Street Journal* bestseller list, number eight overall on all of Amazon, and also became a bestseller on *USA Today*'s bestseller list.

Building on top of that celebrity and fame, Justin has an online course, a best-selling book, a $50,000 investor mastermind, a podcast, and a one-on-one $250,000 a year coaching program. He came to us with no footprint and no content, and we created a new business that generated a million dollars in income in less than 8 months. We also set up impactful connections, built a "strike force" team to handle all the details, and created a ton of buzz, authority, and super credibility in the wealth building and money category. How did we do this from scratch? We leveraged the most appropriate media channels to communicate to his right-fit audience.

In 20 months, the business was over $5.5 million, and less than three years later the business exceeded $15 million in revenue.

Notice how Justin's story unfolded. He knew he was capable of more than he was currently doing (Mindset), but he wasn't sure how to upgrade his business or his brand. I helped him determine the ideal Market and what would be the Model for transformation he would provide (the 10 Commandments of Lifestyle Investing, offered as a course, mastermind, and coaching). Then we identified his Message about lifestyle investing, a phrase that appealed to his ideal client. Finally, we dialed in on the Media, including magazine articles in appropriate publications, a book, a podcast, and more. Yes, it worked — but only because we started with the foundation and built from there.

It bears repeating: Media only works when all the other pieces are in place. And it works better when you layer on the final M, Multipliers.

CH. 7

MULTIPLIERS: TAKING THE ACCELERATORS TO ANOTHER LEVEL

Now we're getting to the really fun stuff. Before we dive in, though, I have to review some basics.

The 6M Growth Accelerators are the core principles that govern everything we do. They have to be followed in order to work properly. One isn't necessarily more important than the others. It's kind of like building a house, to use an already-overused metaphor. You wouldn't say the plumbing is more important than the roof, and the walls are more important than the electrical. But regardless of importance, everything must be done in order, or the final result won't work right.

Multipliers are performance, content creation, and leveraging your knowledge, wisdom, and experience… and then packaging all of that into tools that multiply the value of your offers, brand, reach, and more.

I've spent over 30 years and millions of dollars working with consultants, coaches, advisors, and copywriters building hundreds of Multipliers, and optimizing and hybridizing them. Because there are so many Multipliers, and because I'm developing more all the time, I've included only a sample of them here. (Make sure to follow me on social and sign up for my email list at www.MikeKoenigs.com and podcasts to be informed of the latest additions and updates.)

Think of the rest of this book as a well-stocked spice cabinet. The better your Accelerators, and the more intentional you are in the use of your Multipliers, the better results you'll have. Not every business requires every Multiplier, just like not every recipe needs cilantro or cinnamon. Know what you're going for, and you'll know which Multipliers to select. In some cases, just one Multiplier can be all you need.

All the same, I suggest you read through the whole list. Just reading through them can cause a shift in thinking, and you may be able to adapt or push something you're already doing to another level. We'll start with some of my favorites. Remember, this is just a brief overview of a small sampling of what I pull off the pantry shelves to help my Superpower Accelerator clients. In a future book, I'll include some more, but for now, this should get you started:

30+ MULTIPLIERS to Accelerate Your Business

▶ **Here are a few...**

The Ambassador Method

Referral Parties

Money Phone

The Five Question Close

A Day in the Life

10X Pricing Repackaging

Operation Shock & Awe

The Ambassador Method

Imagine the most trusted person in the world standing in front of your ideal Market and saying, "If you ever get a chance to work with [your name] or [your brand], I'll put my reputation on the line for them." Who would the most trusted person be for you?

Oprah, the Dalai Lama, Tony Robbins, Tiger Woods... who could influence the influencers or affinity groups with one phone call or one relationship?

> **Affinity group: a group of people linked by a common interest or purpose.**

That is the Ambassador Method in a nutshell. It's one of the most powerful transfers of trust and certainty from a trusted authority to YOU. Capitalizing on this one Multiplier alone could generate enough business for the rest of your professional career — or certainly get you in a position where you could sell your business.

Once you know who could really move the needle on your business, ask yourself what Message or story would they need to hear in order to convince them to put their reputation on the line for you? Now, you may not be able to score Tiger or Oprah, but you may not need to.

Think about your perfect customer. Is there an affinity group that these people belong to? Is it EO, YPO, Tiger

21, Vistage, Strategic Coach, Genius Network or some other business networking organization? Maybe it's a trade group. Maybe it's a union. Whatever the group, there's one influencer or leader that all the members trust. That person is your ambassador. That one individual, if they could make a connection for you, give you an endorsement or make a couple of phone calls, could literally eliminate days, weeks, months, or even years of wait time in your sales cycle.

Of course, now you want to know how to reach the Ambassador. What do you say? How do you get them to listen? Do you have to compensate them in some way? etc.

I'm not going to tell you — at least right now. First, it's a detailed process. Second, it's not the point of this book. Instead, this small guide is about giving you an overview of the whole 6M Growth Accelerator process. Then, in future volumes I'll dive into specific elements (including a hand-picked selection of my most powerful Multipliers in specific detail) in future books. How's that for pre-selling?)

Referral Parties

If you don't believe you have a network, you might wonder who you're going to sell your new offers to. Referral Parties are very low-tech solutions. And they're fun to do!

Here's the basic premise. You reach out to people you know. Send them a text or just get them on the phone and say, "Can you and I brainstorm for a minute about one to two people you think could be good referrals?" It's that easy. It's one sentence.

Most people just say yes and give you a name or two, but then I always add, "Anyone else? Is there anyone else?" Most people can think of a couple more people. So, you might walk away with three or four new referrals.

Then, ask them if they'd be willing to make a text introduction on your behalf. That way, you've got their direct contact information. And when your direct connection makes the initial contact, the referral is likely to at least give you an opportunity for the first conversation. Text is preferred — it's way better than email. The message body should be short, direct, and include a link to some form of credibility and copy/paste text that that person can use and forward to someone they can think of. That includes a brief description of you, what you've done, a link to your website, and how to get hold of you.

This works in practically any business. Don't make it too complicated. You're just playing the old "Who do you know…" game with the added element of asking your contact to introduce you right away.

A Day in the Life

How did Elon Musk sell the original $125,000 Tesla Roadster back in 2008? Two words. "Floor it."

When I floored the Tesla Roadster, it went from zero to 60 in 3.7 seconds. I bought that car on the spot. With my jack-o-lantern permagrin on my face, I took the demo car on San Diego's perfect curve — Ardath Road going into La Jolla. The Roadster cemented its position as my favorite toy. I was so inspired that I put solar panels on my roof so I had no gas and no electric bills. Every time I gave someone a ride, they got the uncontrollable "Tesla Grin." Some of the women I took for a ride peed themselves, but everyone said it was better than being on a roller coaster. When the Model S came out, I bought one of those, too.

I share this story, not to brag but to impress upon you the power of experience marketing, what I call A Day in the Life. That's where you answer questions like, *What's it like to work with you? How will they feel? What is the deeper transformation from your product or service? What happens emotionally? What will life be like before, during, and after? How will your lifestyle change?*

Let's say someone visits your website or downloads a PDF, watches a video, or talks to a salesperson. But if they don't say yes, how can you push them over the edge? A piece of Day in the Life content can do that. It is a tool that can be passed along, something that can be used for a follow-up and forwarded after the first contact.

The secret to putting these together is to begin with the transformational captivator. That's a fancy way of saying, "Get a testimonial," but make sure you help your customer tell a story in a way that's usable. Most people are terrible storytellers, and they can't give a good testimonial that's short and effective, so they need some guidance.

Begin by simply asking the subject, "What's it like to be a customer?" Then ask them to share a short backgrounder to add a little bit of credibility and support. And then ask a critical question, which is the reason why they almost didn't join the program. Not, "Why did they buy?" but "Why did they almost NOT buy?" This question doesn't just make for good storytelling. It also will reveal every flaw in your marketing and what the client is really thinking. Next, invite them to share the results they've achieved. From there, transition into step-by-step descriptions of what it's like to be a client. What a day in their life is like and what the outcomes, results, and benefits are. Then, finally, ask them to describe the reason they're willing to share their experiences, and wrap it up by saying that the viewer or reader should buy, too.

Every business should provide some kind of a transformational lifestyle-experience story that features your perfect customer as the hero experiencing a transformation. It makes your brand authentic, raw, and real when done right. (Want to see how I worked with Strategic Coach to create this kind of testimonial? Visit www.MikeKoenigs.com/Go.)

10X Pricing Repackaging

Question: *What's the fastest way to earn a million dollars?*
Answer: *Sell a million-dollar offer to one person.*
Question: *What's the fastest way to make a billion dollars?*
Answer: *Make a billionaire $10 billion and charge a billion.*

The only problem: you need a million-dollar offer or a billion-dollar solution. So what's your highest-priced offer right now? What if you could reprice it at 10X or more without adding more complexity to your business process and keep your expenses the same?

In a previous chapter, I introduced you to Justin Donald. At the time, he was trying to figure out how to package what he did in order to bring in enough money so he and his wife could quit their day jobs. I asked him what he would charge people to teach his system. His response was, "Is $15,000 too much?"

I almost choked, not because it was too much, but because it was too little. I envisioned him teaching already-rich people to do what he did — but they wouldn't be interested at such a low price point. So, we sat down and crafted a $250,000 offer to work one-on-one and a $50,000 group mastermind.

To test it out, the second day we were working together I introduced Justin to a potential client. This guy was a wealthy businessman who had plenty of cash, had made some bad investments and lost money, and wanted to find a better way. After a short conversation, Justin made the enrollment for $250,000, and a week later someone else he knew also enrolled. That's $500,000 in a matter of a week — the equivalent of more than 33 clients at the $15,000 price point. How long do you think it would have taken Justin to find 33 $15,000 clients? A lot more than a week!

I talked to Justin recently and he was ready to raise his prices even higher. "I'm too busy!" he said. He's on his way to a million-dollar offer. You can be, too, when your Mindset is right and you pinpoint the exact Market, Model, and Message.

Operation Shock & Awe

Your mission, should you choose to accept it, is to absolutely blow your prospective client's mind at the first point of contact so there is absolutely zero chance they could forget you. Be so unique and different that you are permanently etched into their mind and heart forever.

Imagine receiving a FedEx box. You open it up and inside is an iPad. Attached to it is a $100 bill and a Post-it note with the message, "I have a quick favor to ask. Turn on the iPad and press play for a two-minute video from me to see how we can 5X your business. Regardless if we work together, the iPad and money are yours." At the end of that video, a message says, "If you'd like to know more, let's have a 10-minute phone call. Reach me any time at (858) 412-0858."

That package would likely not only get past your receptionist, assistant, or other gatekeeper, but it would also get your attention. And I'd bet way more than $100 that you would at least start watching the video.

This is just one example of Shock and Awe. My good friend John Ruhlin wrote a book on giving memorable gifts called Giftology. (You can listen to the podcast episode I did with him here: www.mikekoenigs.com/how-to-be-unforgettable-and-get-the-most-profitable-clients/) He has amazing stories about using remarkable gifts to get people's attention and build relationships.

One of his best stories is about a mutual friend who did some work with Tony Robbins and wanted to give him something unforgettable. So, John created a set of custom knives, each of which is engraved with one of Tony's quotes. And inside this custom carved box was a video screen with my friend thanking Tony personally for the opportunity to get to know him and work with him. Tony's wife, Sage, actually reached out to my buddy and thanked him personally for such a remarkable gift and said it was one of the nicest, most memorable things they'd ever received and they'd cherish it forever. That is Shock and Awe.

You don't have to spend hundreds or thousands of dollars. Creativity counts more than cost. The key is grabbing attention, creating intrigue, building trust, all of which a gift does.

You can stack this strategy with some of the others. If you don't have the relationships, you can get them from referrals, the Ambassador Method, or some of the other audience-building multipliers I've created. Your key is to get your foot in the door, elevate your status authority, collapse the trust barrier, and start a conversation.

These are just five brief overviews among the dozens upon dozens of other Multipliers I've successfully used for my businesses, as well as for my Superpower Accelerator private clients. Stay tuned; I'll be sharing more in the future.

CH. 8

NEXT STEPS FOR YOUR CATEGORY OF ONE BRAND

This book is based on over 30 years of experience, generating over $100 million for myself and my clients, developing million-dollar products, offers, and pitches. Its purpose is not to give you a complete, step-by-step process to follow, but to provide a high-level view of the type of transformation that is possible for you. If you want to create an exceptional business and an exceptional life, this guide can help you see what's possible.

If you're ready for the next step, there are a number of ways we can work together.

The Superpower Accelerator Workshop

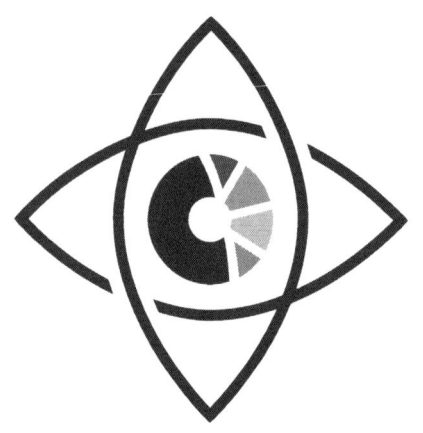

If you want to differentiate yourself from your competitors, attract highly valuable prospects who trust you and pay you what you deserve, repel people who waste your time, and impact people's lives with your expertise, I invite you to apply for an experience that could change the foundation of you as an entrepreneur as well as your business from this point forward. It's called the Superpower Accelerator. Together with my team, we'll turn your creative vision into a product, promotion, and REINVENT YOU and your business in just three days.

Not only will you learn valuable skills, talents, and capabilities during that time, but you'll also take those wins back to your team and impact your businesses.

If this sounds like something you want to take advantage of, the next step is to visit www.MikeKoenigs.com/Go to book a call with me. You can also send an email to VIP@PaidForLife.com, text (858) 412-0858, or send a homing pigeon with a little note affixed to this front talon, saying, "Mike, I'm ready to get the hell out of my own way, reinvent my business, create a breakthrough in my profitability, and experience the big wins and gains I'm meant to."

Masterminds

Several times per year I invite clients I'm working with, people I want to work with, and thought leaders to come together for exotic and fun masterminds. Some of them are focused on Life Extension where we get full body and brain scans, meet with peptide and hormone experts, and get exposed to the latest in life extension technology and tools.

Another one was focused on cryptocurrency trading, investing, and the creation of NFTs. We traveled with a sommelier and a celebrity chef and stayed at a remarkable compound in Guadalupe Valley, Mexico, home of over 300 wineries and some of the best food in the world.

Spouses are encouraged to join, and we dig deep into relationships, life extension, psychology, trauma, and of course business. I like to say, "welcome to the family you choose, not the one you were born into."

If you fit the "Perfect Customer" profile we discussed in Chapter 3, Market, you're probably a right-fit for this very limited experience. Learn more and apply at www.MikeKoenigs.com/MM.

The Superpower Accelerator Blueprint

If you have a team that's ready and able to support you through your reinvention process and want a guide that you can use, The Superpower Accelerator Blueprint is a DIY version of the Superpower Accelerator Workshop.

The kit is jam-packed with templates, worksheets, and examples to help you work through the 6M Growth Accelerators while you create your *Category of One* brand. While not as personalized and powerful as the in-person Workshop experience (and you'll miss out on those ocean views!), The Superpower Accelerator Blueprint provides an in-depth look at applying the 6M Growth Accelerators to your own business and life.

Find out more at www.MikeKoenigs.com/Blueprint.

Podcasts

I produce two weekly podcasts designed to grow your business and improve your mindset.

The "Capability Amplifier" podcast is about sharing useful, intellectual shortcuts, with the smartest man in business, Dan Sullivan, founder of Strategic Coach. Most episodes are typically only Dan and me, but we occasionally interview fascinating guests like Suzy Batiz (founder of Poo Pourri), investor Steve Jurvetson, Shari Salata, Gino Wickman, Jason Flom, Yakov Smirnoff, Adam Conover and other fascinating guests — www.MrBz.com/CA

I host a second podcast, "The Big Leap," with Gay Hendricks, a multiple *New York Times* bestselling author and a

Next Steps for Your Category of One Brand | 113

coaches' coach. The focus is on the decisions in life that change everything and the "Upper Limits" challenge every high performer deals with. You can check it out at www.MrBz.com/BL.

MEET MIKE KOENIGS

Mike Koenigs is a true Renaissance man. Filmmaker; serial entrepreneur; VC and angel investor; judge on Entrepreneur.com's *Elevator Pitch*; *Forbes*, *Fast Company*, and *Entrepreneur* writer; and 13-time bestselling author. He co-hosts two podcasts, "Capability Amplifier" with Strategic Coach's Dan Sullivan and "The Big Leap" with NYT Bestselling author, Gay Hendricks.

He has coached, advised, and sold products and services to over 161,000 business owners in virtually every industry including Sony, BMW, General Mills, 3M. His celebrity clients include Tony Robbins, Paula Abdul, Richard Dreyfuss, Dave Asprey, John Assaraf, Brian Tracy, Peter Diamandis, Daniel Amen, and Darren Hardy. His latest venture, "The Superpower Accelerator," works with founders to create, launch, and monetize new businesses and products.

BOOK MIKE KOENIGS TO SPEAK

Book Mike as your Keynote Speaker and You're Guaranteed to Make Your Event Inspirational, Motivational, Highly Entertaining, and Unforgettable!

For nearly three decades, Mike Koenigs has been educating, entertaining, motivating, and inspiring entrepreneurs to start, scale, and sell their businesses and reinvent themselves for their 2nd acts, 3rd acts, and beyond.

His origin story includes his recent near-death brush with stage 3a cancer, growing up lower middle-class in a small town in Eagle Lake, Minnesota, severe ADHD, and "meeting" Tony

Robbins through an infomercial that changed his life forever. After successfully building and exiting from two companies and selling them to publicly-traded companies, Mike can share relevant, actionable strategies that anyone can use — even if they're starting from scratch.

His unique style inspires, empowers, and entertains audiences while giving them the tools and strategies they need and want to get seen and heard to build and grow successful sustainable brands and businesses.

For more info and to book Mike for your next event, visit www.MikeKoenigs.com/Speaking or call +1 (858) 412-0858.

Join the Mastermind

THE SUPERPOWER ACCELERATOR MASTERMIND SERIES

Destination Retreats with an Entrepreneurial Purpose.

Apply to join an exclusive group of **future-focused**, **high-achieving**, **abundance-minded** founders and entrepreneurs.

SUPERPOWER ACCELERATOR

MikeKoenigs.com/MM

Create a Business You'll Love for the Rest of Your Life

GET YOUR 10X MULTIPLIER BLUEPRINT

A 7-Figure Brand, Offer, & Message-Building Workshop in a Box

PACKED WITH WORKSHEETS, GUIDES, TEMPLATES, AND MORE!

MikeKoenigs.com/Blueprint

SUPERPOWER ACCELERATOR